DEVELOPING GOLFERS INTO PLAYERS

John Perna
Founder & President
TPS Player Service

Cover and text design by Sea Script Company/Apostle's Landing

Cover and text layout by Sea Script Company/Apostle's Landing

Illustrations by Rayah James and Sea Script Company

Sea Script Company

Seattle, Washington

www.seascriptcompany.com

206.390.6628

info@seascriptcompany.com

ISBN: 978-1-7335583-0-3

Library of Congress Control Number: 2018964192

First Printing January 2019

Printed in the United States

SEA SCRIPT COMPANY
BOOK PUBLISHING

Dedicated to the original golf parents (my parents),
Mike and Adelle

https://tpsplayerservice.com

[Note: QR Codes are used to link you to the video site pictured. You can download a free QR Code Scanner to your smartphone through the App Store/Play Store on your phone
or
You can access the video by typing into the internet the website address shown.]

CONTENTS

FOREWORD
Chip Brewer
CEO, Callaway Golf

My connection to John Perna, and the 10-year friendship that has resulted from it, happened through Dr. Jim Suttie. My father is an accomplished player, two-time USGA Senior Amateur champion Gordon Brewer, and Doc Suttie is a longtime family friend. One day more than a decade ago, we were in Florida hitting balls on the range and Doc was there teaching. John was working with him, mainly as a clubfitter, so we were introduced.

If you were interested in golf performance and training and you fell into a conversation with John, especially back then, you knew right away he was working on some new and very cutting-edge ideas. I remember being impressed by the originality of his player-development concepts, but equally so by his obvious passion and commitment. I came away thinking he was a golf coach ahead of his time, and sensing that John would have a significant influence on the teaching profession.

And that's turned out to be the case. In my role as CEO of Callaway Golf, I get to see and hear the game's top experts on player performance, and it's clear that the coaching world is moving in John's direction. Things are evolving quickly in this field and the Player Service, John's academy, is helping lead the way. I expect more and more of the people who coach elite talent to adopt many of the techniques and beliefs that TPS has pioneered.

They will have to do it in their own individual way, of course. John's personal style would be difficult for anyone to copy. He is demanding of his students in a way that is only possible if you care deeply about each player as a human being. As you'll learn by reading the stories they tell in these pages, John's players are constantly being shown the future. They hear from John about talents and inner strength no young person can know they possess until an adult with unique powers of perception and a deep belief in human potential spots it.

Of course, there is a flip side to that, well-known to anyone who's capable of viewing life realistically. The flip side is that we can let ourselves down when we lose the inner will to persevere and lose our passion for finding out just how far we can go in our journey.

The stories in this book include many moments in which honest, frank commentary from the coach is greatly needed for a young athlete to see where they're stuck and what they're missing about the reality of their situation. The ability to give that message so that it stings but it doesn't wound—instead it supports the young person to find a new level of energy and self-belief—is a gift that's very rare, especially today. Listen to TPS golfers describe their experiences, and you'll come across such profound moments pretty frequently.

John's golf academy is located in Chicago and I'm raising my family in Southern California. If not for that, my youngest son would be training with John at TPS. It's a place where the golf swing is understood to be about athleticism, speed, strength, power and agility. Our engineering team at Callaway Golf, for the most part, is inspired by what our clubs and balls can produce in the hands of players who emerge from training programs like John's. There are also times when we wonder how much we'll have to rethink club design, in order to accommodate the new athleticism in our sport!

The game of golf isn't just about golf swings, however. No coaching philosophy accepts this fact more than John's. At TPS, athleticism in golf extends to the body's metabolism, the visual system, self-awareness, situational judgment, even to what's in a player's heart as it beats faster in competition. All those factors are vital because they contribute to the full attainment of an individual athlete's potential, which in my view is the core concept of the Player Service.

PREFACE
How to Read This Book
Dr. Rick Jensen
Coach, Sport Psychologist, Author

The field of golf instruction is undergoing rapid change, due in large part to emerging technology. In the U.S. and other advanced countries, new technology comes to market at a rapid rate. Whoever is going to apply it must understand its benefits and spot any possible drawbacks.

This is just the right time for John Perna's book, *Developing Golfers into Players*, to come along. The beliefs and instincts that guide John as a coach represent an ideal way of working with the high-tech diagnostics that have quickly become vital to instruction and training. Compared to past eras, information we could only guess at now appears on-screen in vast quantities. Despite the obvious value of this information, it requires a similar advancement in the science and art of actual golfer training, customized to the individual player. This is my professional opinion and having known John for many years, I know he shares it.

John has been in the vanguard of coaches who acknowledge the value of knowing what happens in the golf swing even while devising new, artful ways to guide students through the real-life process of upgrading physical performance. That's the true challenge of this era—learning all we can about the brain-body connection and then creatively devising practice protocols that consider how individual athletes acquire not just motor skills but the ability to successfully execute motor performance.

Think a moment about practice on the range and competition on the course, and you'll recognize the difference between acquiring motor skills and improving motor performance. There's a fine example of how the individual player can benefit from this distinction in the chapter on "The Advantage of Periodization," narrated by one of John's players, Dan Hudson.

In that chapter and others, you'll also see how vital it is for coaches to go beyond swing mechanics and basic on-course decision-making to address the complex emotional makeup of the golfer, especially the teenage golfer. And this must be done with impeccable honesty and compassion, qualities you'll see exhibited throughout this book.

Indeed, its pages are filled with narratives that reveal John's capacities to connect, to build trust, to diagnose what's going on and to inventively construct custom training programs. His highly specialized skill set has helped no fewer than 80 junior players from the Player Service, or TPS, reach their goal of becoming Division 1 NCAA golfers *in just eight years.* That's a pretty amazing record, especially for a startup training facility tucked in the Chicago suburbs, not some long-established academy in the warm climate of Florida.

From the beginning of his career, John has been intuitively aware of a growing distinction between presenting people with data and training them to acquire advanced golf skills. The latter are the type of skills that translate directly to low scores and high tournament finishes. Years ago, when John first became exposed to my teachings—my doctorate is in Sport Psychology and Exercise Science—he was gratified to learn that there is scholarship to back up his keen instincts.

Our job as golf coaches is not to teach golf, but to facilitate the learning of golf so that our players never get mechanics-bound or result-bound. Data overload and an emphasis on static positions serves to take the athleticism away, when what we ought to be doing is creating conditions that allow self-discovery about dynamic motion.

There is very little being written or shared about this combination of art and science in golf coaching, which is why I'm so certain John's book will be well-received. Indeed, an entire chapter, narrated by TPS alumnus Joo-Young Lee, is devoted to the theme of self-discovery for elite golfers. Another chapter, about making sure the athlete doesn't become stripped of his or her athleticism, is told in the voice of TPS player Robert Renner, a long-time hockey player who switched sports late in his adolescence but still made it as a Division 1 NCAA golfer.

Which brings up an important point about the structure of this book and the philosophy guiding it. It is through the voices of the young people he has coached in the Player Service that John's insights are described and his process of turning the talented golfer into a true tournament player is revealed. I find this to be a brilliant way to write this book and present its ideas. Why? Because the true test of a great teacher is their ability to teach students a complete conceptual knowledge of a subject. On that basis, I believe through his students' voices you will see what a phenomenal job John's training system does at equipping students with complete ownership of the core TPS concepts. In addition, I am certain you will find these young people to be excellent storytellers. The 11 who contributed chapters are the true "first generation" of TPS, students who were in the program all the way through high school and college.

In the early stages of planning this book, John decided to partner with veteran golf journalist David Gould, author of several books on golf including a definitive history of the PGA Tour Qualifying Tournament (or "Q School") and arranged for David to conduct lengthy interviews with the players.

That process included an interview with one other important source, veteran golf coach Dan Kochevar, John's former instructor and the father of two TPS players whose stories also became part of this book. The result of all the research and writing is a highly intriguing view of what it's like for junior golfers to go through TPS training and navigate, with academy support, the challenges of the NCAA recruitment process and the rigors of NCAA competition.

John was a good enough player to compete on professional tours, and a smart enough student of the game to see how different elite coaching was from a standard golf lesson. That's what got him started on the path he has blazed for nearly a decade. What you'll find in his book is a highlight reel of the discoveries and innovations that are lifting John Perna to the heights of his profession and guiding the progress of his appreciative students through their remarkable careers in high school and college golf, even as it helps prepare them for the life challenges they choose to take on further down the road.

INTRODUCTION
How the TPS Concept Came to Be
John Perna

The essence of knowledge is self-knowledge.

— Plato

Throughout life we are confronted with many difficult questions but none more daunting than "What is my purpose?" This question haunts me, and through a long period of self-reflection I've come to believe that the purpose of life on this planet is to master one's self. I also believe you learn to do that through learning to master your passion. In turn, learning to master your passion serves as a metaphor for what it will take to truly know oneself. These two motivations explain why I built TPS.

Think about any worthwhile activity that is difficult to master. Whether it's a sport or a craft or an art form or maybe some type of survival skill, there are various ways you could try to become good at it. You could devote yourself to learning it on your own. You could find a fellow learner and the two of you could teach each other or at least encourage each other. You could find an expert and hire that person to teach you, or you could combine the benefits of all those approaches and immerse yourself in a community of skill-learners, training as a group under the guidance of someone with relevant expertise.

Player Service is a company, but I think of it more as a community. In fact, if TPS wasn't designed as a community and was not organized to bring students and coaches together in a personal way, I doubt it would succeed as a company. One of the reasons it wouldn't succeed is that I wouldn't be very motivated to manage it. I'm not much interested in golf skill development that's organized around the traditional one-on-one format. My strong preference is to develop talented junior golfers in a communal environment because that type of environment encourages self-discovery and self-discovery is the essential ingredient to accelerated learning.

Having played Division 1 NCAA golf, and for a brief while professional golf, I often found myself in the traditional role of the student—taking lessons, listening, nodding my head, getting some guidance, then going off to hit balls.

I've also found myself in the opposite role, as golf instructor and coach. But from the very beginning, I did something else, something in-between: I spent long hours in the role of observer. Traditional golf instruction is based on the so-called private lesson, but in practice golf is not like piano or sailing. When you're finished taking a private golf lesson and you choose not to pack up and head home, you can hang around and watch the next person's lesson, which is what I always did.

I would stand off to the side, just within earshot, to study the golfer and the coach working together. And I didn't do it to kill time until one of my parents came by to pick me up. In fact, if they were coming to pick me up, I would hope they got delayed at work or stuck in traffic. I was fascinated watching the golfer swing, listening for the impact, watching ball flight, watching the student's reaction, listening to the coach's comments and trying to guess or imagine what he might say next.

When a lesson was over, I'd be curious whether the student chose to practice the movement or drill the instructor gave him, or whether he practiced at all. Young golf instructors who ask advice on how best to improve in their craft are often told to go watch good teachers teach. But no one ever gave me that suggestion. They didn't have to because I was instinctually doing it from day one.

If you do this habitually over a long span of time, you eventually run into at least a few other people who do the same thing. Fellow "range rats," you might say. But really, it's only natural to get pleasure out of watching someone else travel up a learning curve and develop refined skills. It's part of the bonding that takes place as our students train together. Now, golf isn't thought of as a team sport, since at the professional level 99% of all competitions are individual. But that doesn't mean we can't introduce a powerful element of community and togetherness into the golf-improvement experience. You can do it very successfully with juniors and you can do it just as effectively with adults. Dr. Rick Jensen, who wrote the Preface to this book, has an ever-growing list of high-echelon golf instructors who have picked up on his viewpoint that learning and practicing in groups makes far more sense than doing it on an individual basis.

This concept really hit home with me as I was studying the evolution of the American motorcycle business. An uncle of mine is a motorcycle enthusiast who knows quite a bit about the history of the industry, which he would often share with me. Naturally, Uncle Ed had a particular interest in Harley-Davidson, and he got me interested in their story, as well. Most people don't realize that for decades Harley ranked No. 2 in U.S. manufacturing to the leading brand, which was Indian. Even as Harley-Davidson managed to build bikes that were just as fast or faster than Indian-built bikes, they still couldn't compete with the brand equity Indian had built.

Then the company hit upon a strategy—establish motorcycle clubs open only to Harley purchasers. The idea was to bring together like-minded riders who would share their common passion. These clubs became more critical to business-building than the bikes themselves because they created something much bigger—community! It was yet another proof of Aristotle's premise that the whole is greater than the sum of its parts. In this case, the Harley motorcycle and its owners were parts that, because of the club idea, had become a whole worth much more. This concept is what TPS was built on and continues to be the building block that makes us grow and succeed.

Along those same lines, the genius of PGA Junior League Golf is that it finally turned golf into a true team sport at the youth level with team members wearing matching shirts and enjoying the same camaraderie and positive energy we associate with soccer, basketball or any of the major team sports. It took a long time to make this discovery, but eventually the light bulb went on. Proven fact: If you understand the power of group energy and you make it available to junior golfers at the top of the talent pyramid, you create a continuing-education mechanism that leads to true mastery. Let me circle back to something mentioned previously when I referred to the one-on-one golf lesson that ends with a kid packing up his sticks and going home. To me that is a truly sad sight and a crucial lost opportunity. TPS is set up to be diametrically opposed to that scenario.

As you'll learn in the first chapter, the other key to TPS, besides our community-based learning environment, is the way our training follows a carefully and thoroughly designed system, sub-divided into specific segments. Because we have turned out more than 80 Division 1 NCAA golfers, we get a fair number of golf coaches coming to visit us and to observe our training system. Not long ago a visiting college golf coach saw me working with a player, eventually giving him a drill to practice. When that session was over, the player made dramatic progress and the visiting coach wanted to ask me about the drill, how it was designed and so forth. His assumption was that the drill, or the words I used to describe it, is what led the student to his quick improvement.

That's natural enough, but I feel it misses the point. Every competent golf coach has effective drills they give to their students. At TPS we call these "tools in your toolbox." And although the tools (drills) have merit, we believe the learning environment supersedes any drill or training tool and thus is the fundamental cause of efficient learning. We work hard to educate our players on separating what we believe to be fundamentals and tools in their toolbox for executing a task. A fundamental is something you must do to be successful at a particular skill and a tool is something you can use to execute those fundamentals. It's my view that a lack of understanding of this concept is what causes most coaches and golfers to fall short of their potential.

So we have built a training system and our players come to know it very well. Our training system is what separates TPS from other golf academies. One aspect of the system involves correct hierarchy or sequencing in the use of technology, for example, Trackman. In order to become TPS students in the first place, one must attain a grade of 90 or above on a certification test and write a five-page essay, all about the system. Although students are all different, the sequence and systematic interpretation of the data is the same for all. This allows our players to get into their fix—their adjustment—quickly and easily. TPS players are constantly seeing that sequence being followed. They study each other's process. The students buy in because they not only see their own results, they also observe all their fellow students achieving tremendous success. As a result, the community becomes the system.

DEVELOPING GOLFERS INTO PLAYERS

Kyle proves that possessing the attributes of a great coach supersedes the intricate knowledge of mechanics. He is the example I point to in describing how our system can expedite the learning process for coaches as well as players. Kyle is indeed one of the game's top young coaches, and I'm thrilled that he was the first coach ever to be certified in Developing Golfers into Players.

—J.P.

1

CAN A BASEBALL COACH BECOME A GREAT GOLF COACH?

KYLE SLECHTA

Having been part of the Player Service from the beginning—as a coach, not a player—I have a unique perspective on its inner workings. What's interesting about me is I have no training in golf instruction or in clubfitting beyond what I've learned through TPS. I'm not a member of the PGA, and I never took part in the PGA Apprentice program. I was a baseball player in high school and college, then an assistant baseball coach, so the opportunity to go through PGA training never presented itself.

Having zero golf experience beyond the fact that I played the game recreationally, I provided John with a blank slate. My background in athletics and education, my work ethic and my communication skills were what I brought to the table. From that starting point, whatever John taught me would be the sum total of what I would know about helping people improve as golfers. That's the way he wanted it. I wouldn't have to un-learn anything.

I was drawn to TPS by its unique atmosphere and by the results it was getting. After a short time there, my plans for teaching school and coaching baseball, work I had trained for over many years, began to fade. Of the first seven players to come through John's system—Kyle Kochevar, Tee-K Kelly, Brian Bullington, Charlie Netzel, Daniel Hudson, David Cooke and Joe Carlson—six of them would end up earning PGA Tour-affiliated professional status by the age of 24. That's a phenomenal success rate and if you were there in the early days, you could sense it happening. As for that seventh player, Joe Carlson, he would end up going to law school.

Any fine coach can produce two or three very good players, but TPS has produced an astoundingly high number of them, in a cold northerly climate, drawing students from a 20-mile radius. That defies all odds, and I witnessed it unfolding month by month, season by season. So I knew very quickly that I wanted to make TPS my professional home.

Of course, "professional" means you do something for pay, perhaps even make a living at it. At the start, the Player Service didn't generate enough money to support even one coach, let alone two. That meant having to work extra jobs to meet living expenses, which was fine with me. I did some private coaching with high school baseball players, and I worked a lot of shifts in a delicatessen my dad owns. But I could see the success of TPS building. The company is now to the point where it generates over a million dollars a year in revenue. The decision to be part of TPS has meant success for me financially and rapid development of my coaching ability and reputation.

I first got a sense of John's expertise in golf after he fit me for a set of clubs, then custom-built them using his proprietary system for shaft selection and frequency matching. I took that set of clubs to a series of well-regarded clubfitters, and none of them could come up with anything remotely as good. One of the fitters kept me in his studio half the afternoon trying to figure out what John had done.

Of our first seven players. . .six of them would end up earning PGA Tour-affiliated professional status by the age of 24.

A while later, as we continued working together, John asked me to read *The Talent Code* by Daniel Coyle, which made a big impression on me. It allowed me to see how TPS was naturally developing a "talent hotbed" just by drawing on local juniors and training them in a sport you can only play seven months a year here in Chicago. The way the golfers who have been part of our hotbed relate to each other and go through training together was another intriguing aspect of TPS, especially to someone like me who had played a team sport for so long and played it at a high level.

John's approach is to build systems for everything. There is a formal TPS System for driving, iron play, wedges, putting, clubfitting, putter-fitting, green-reading, optimal brain performance, course management and a few others. All of these systems are a by-product of the education John received from all of his work with the top certification programs. He is certified in pretty much anything a golf coach would want to learn but, as I've discovered over the years, there is a difference between simply having the certifications and having advanced systems. The goal of our training in ball striking and shot making is to shrink the player's dispersion pattern, both long and short and from left to right. That's a mantra for us.

Even though what we do looks simple, it's complex in the sense that so much experimentation had to happen for the system to emerge in its present form. One early breakthrough was the system for interpreting Trackman data and going directly into a hierarchy of steps and corrections that is proprietary to TPS. Someone who is certified in the TPS System will know just where to start no matter what problem the student is having. And so, despite arriving here with no training in golf, I was able to quickly start helping players. I've never been certified in Trackman but once I learned the TPS driving system, I knew how to work backwards from the data and was able to get a player hitting the ball with a pure strike in a short span of time, measurable in minutes.

Our players end up competing in lots of tournaments, and because we accompany them to select events, I've spent many afternoons on practice ranges at tournament sites. This has given me an opportunity to observe techniques and approaches that non-TPS coaches follow. I've observed many well-regarded coaches taking Trackman data and using it to help their students fine-tune their driving or scoring shots. I've seen where they start, and it isn't where we would start. I've seen how long it takes them to generate a change in the player's movement pattern, and I've known with certainty how much less time it would take using the TPS System. I've stood watching for a very long time and have seen examples of the coach never actually getting to the fix that's needed. At this point in my career and with my limited background, I should not be able to watch a plus-5 handicap professional struggle with his driver and know that I'm capable of getting him straightened out in short order. But I'm certified in the TPS System, and that system makes a lot of things possible.

Time is the most valuable commodity in the world. You can't get it back. The system we use at TPS is all about fixing the mechanical flaws as fast as possible. We operate on a business model that requires a year-long commitment by the player and his or her family so we're motivated to get the swing issues fixed as fast as possible. We're "Developing Golfers into Players," as our tagline explains, and that doesn't happen for a player when he or she is going through a swing change. *Golfers don't get better when they are working on their mechanics.* They start to get better once the mechanical issues are dealt with.

We don't ration out our guidance on the swing fix over time, as sometimes happens in golf instruction. We get past the initial work on mechanics as quickly as we can so that we can move the player along into tangible skill building. For example, our wedge system is their chance to learn to control what we call "horizontal and vertical clubface contact with the ball" as well as "control the physics of launch" with their wedges. Despite how important that training is, we still endeavor to breeze through it so the player can spend the majority of their time on building the skill of controlling carry distance and spin with the wedges.

At TPS, we don't believe in tips because we don't believe in some kind of secret inside knowledge or magic bullet that turns faulty swings into great swings. We don't want to get in the way of a player's natural athleticism, which comes when they are in a flow state not a thinking state. If a coach believes that his value to players lies in having a long list of tips or suggestions to share, he is liable to give them to the wrong people at the wrong times. It's an approach that can lead to the scenario where a player is assigned a four-week practice program based on one of these tips or swing keys with no guarantee it's appropriate.

If you were to come and observe TPS training, you might be surprised at how seldom we use verbal cues like "Release it from the top" or "Fire your hips." We say things like that as little as possible. Nine times out of ten we're observing, and the player is finding their own way to achieve a certain fix. The only time we'll interrupt that process is if the player is losing speed or trying to solve a problem with a fix that will create another problem. Otherwise, they find their own cues and their own athletic pathway to the good result.

For John, this is a case of our players doing what Byron Nelson did or Ben Hogan or Bobby Jones except there is technology to guide them. Technology has revolutionized golf coaching and accelerated the learning process because it provides the player and coach with accurate feedback. If they have the right system for using it, they never take steps backward and they avoid hours of work on the wrong thing. Within TPS, talking by coaches and cognitive thinking by players are each minimized. We can bring about a correct ground-force reaction and bio-mechanically sound swing movements without asking the student to rely on conscious swing thoughts.

The goal is always to free up a player's natural athleticism with technology supporting that aim.

Our training system moves the player along from an assessment based on metrics to their own intuitive sense of how to change what's happening, then on to drills and competitive tests, interspersed with more measurements. After years of refinements based on constant trial and error, TPS training has put that architecture in place. TPS players can therefore work toward mastery of their mechanics without ever "getting mechanical." We give them a platform and rules that map out the learning process and, as a result, are able to accelerate it. The goal is always to free up a player's natural athleticism with technology supporting that aim.

Every golfer has a natural, genetic movement pattern; you can think of it as a "movement thumbprint." It will come to the forefront as a matter of course. We want a TPS student's corrections to happen within that natural movement pattern in a way that respects basic physics and lets them be as efficient as possible. At the same time, we make certain there is a feel factor that goes along with all their corrected movement patterns. Only when they can connect a physical sensation to the adjustment we're asking for are we on to the next step. We find that the students are very capable of recognizing how their adjustments feel.

Every golfer has a natural, genetic movement pattern; you can think of it as a "movement thumbprint."

We teach in accordance with brain centers and how they function. TPS players are guided through a process designed to activate the cerebellum and quiet the prefrontal cortex. The cerebellum is where signals from the body's sensory systems and the spinal cord get sent. It's how humans regulate their motor movements, and smooth out those movements, working toward ideal balance. Many a golfer has created problems for himself by letting the prefrontal cortex become very engaged while a swing change is pursued. When you're trying to learn a motor skill, you don't want a lot of activity in the prefrontal cortex. That's the part of your brain that's devoted to complex cognitive behavior, personality expression, decision making and social interaction.

At the TPS indoor facility outside of Chicago, no expense has been spared in putting together a full arsenal of technology.

The center is equipped with three Trackman simulator bays, a Science and Motion PuttLab, a PuttView augmented-reality putting green and a FocusBand Brain Training Headset and Performance App. This is a key part of the TPS System—it lets the player use technology to improve their game without thinking mechanics.

Visitors always comment on how John laid out the facility: There are no dividers between hitting stations and the putting green is wide open to the hitting bays. Literally, there is no privacy. That's another example of John's emphasis on a community of learning. Having no dividers helps foster the competitive environment. It's supportively competitive, to put a finer point on it, which accelerates progress. As mentioned previously, a golfer who is "working on mechanics" in the traditional way won't make much improvement according to what John has concluded from all his experimentation. Improvement comes from working on mindsets and skills sets, especially competitively, and using what you gain in that process to lower your score.

Having your technology and knowing basically how it works just gets you started. Within an optimal system, there needs to be a hierarchy of steps and procedures that works fundamentally, across the board, yet is also diverse and fluid and easy to adapt to for individual players and coaches.

Education is paramount at TPS and is a foundation of the TPS System. Every player here is educated enough to make an informed decision about important stages of their training. Being a TPS certified coach means having the ability to not only understand the information and help golfers play better, it's about being able to educate players in a comprehensive manner to internalize the science of the TPS System.

Likely as not, a TPS student who sees a particular drill being done will understand it, or try to understand it, in the context of "neutralization." There are many facets and building blocks of the TPS training system, but neutralization is one of the core concepts. It's a lens through which those who know our system view any particular piece of training. You'll learn quite a bit about our approach to neutralization as you read this book, particularly the chapter that is narrated by Kyle Kochevar. All but a few of this book's chapters are narrated by students who have come through TPS and been part of the community. That's only right, since the personal experience of the students is the essence of what takes place here.

> TPS truly is becoming a center of golf equipment research, along with being a leading academy.

Clubfitting is also a big factor in all this. I've sat in on many a meeting John has held with major club manufacturers. On multiple occasions, I've heard top executives or veteran engineers thank him for sharing information about shaft performance and club performance that was new to them despite all their expertise in the subject. They see him as possessing a rare understanding of the gap between club design or club manufacturing and the coaching/training process, and knowing how to bridge that gap. One CEO of a prominent shaft company told John in all seriousness that he was "the smartest person he's ever spoken to in the golf industry." TPS truly is becoming a center of golf equipment research, along with being a leading academy. The 2017-18 period has been particularly productive. There is a new golf shaft coming out of John's design shop and a putting-fitting system that changes face angle and path just through the fitting.

At the core of the TPS fitting system, we fit our players (and refit them, on a continual basis) to golf equipment that produces optimal ball flight when the optimal movements are made, and produces very sub-optimal ball flight otherwise. "If you make bad swings, I want to see bad ball flight" is a phrase you'll hear John say quite often. That undesirable ball flight is great information. It's feedback that forces a golfer to make the swing that gets physics working in their favor.

All these ingredients that add up to tournament success are described in many of the chapters that follow, chapters that are narrated by a TPS player who came through the system, grew, developed, learned, gained maturity and came to deeply appreciate the friendship and camaraderie of the other members of the "talent hotbed" known as TPS.

I have been very fortunate to work with them and get to know them. I think you'll enjoy getting to know these exceptional young men and women as well. Before that series of student-narrated chapters, there's a quick history of how and why TPS came into being. To explain all that, we turn to someone who knows it well, the highly regarded swing instructor Dan Kochevar.

TPS Elite Video
https://www.youtube.com/watch?v=aoc2lpiWryU&t=4s

Dan Kochevar and I first crossed paths in 1997 when I went to him for golf lessons. Our two decades of friendship and collaboration have been greatly rewarding to me. It's fairly common now for young golf professionals to choose instruction as a specialty and make teaching their career, but it was pretty rare when Dan went that route. He made the right decision, as his success and his pride in his work clearly show. Eventually the tables were turned, in a sense, with Dan sending his son Kyle to me for coaching. Because he was there at the beginning of TPS—and indeed long before the beginning—I asked Dan to explain how it all came to be. He said he would give it a try, and this chapter is the result.

— J.P.

2

"DIG IT
OUT OF
THE DIRT"

The Player Service was created in 2010. In the short time since, TPS has achieved what I consider to be an unprecedented level of success. In just that eight-year period, TPS has sent more than 80 players off to play Division 1 collegiate golf, meanwhile training multiple junior and collegiate All-Americans. TPS Elite is a golf academy for elite juniors aiming to play collegiate golf, college golfers aspiring to play professionally and professional golfers who dream of playing the PGA Tour and LPGA Tour. It is unique in its programs and training styles.

The funny part is that it almost never came to be. In 2010, the global economy was in a serious recession and the idea of starting any high-end business was farfetched at best. I can remember one winter day that year talking with John Perna about his vision to build a golf

DAN KOCHEVAR

training academy exclusively for the tournament player. As John presented the idea, it began to seem, not only viable, but compelling. I encouraged him to seek the advice of other successful golf instructors and business owners to further develop his plan. John said he had done that very thing, and the people he spoke to weren't encouraging. "They all think I'm nuts" is how John phrased it. But I saw the value in what he envisioned. I knew there was a need for something like TPS.

> His vision is to build a golf training academy exclusively for the tournament player.

I've been a PGA professional for 20-plus years and have been exclusively teaching golf as my own boss for the majority of that time. In the 1980s when I left Medinah Country Club to go out on my own, I too was considered not quite sane by my peers. In my case, it proved to be the right decision, as I have built a thriving golf teaching business and pursued the career I knew would make me happy.

The more I listened to John and grasped his concepts, both on the operation of a golf academy and the training of elite golfers, the more I realized how cutting-edge his plan and his thinking were. I believed that specializing in such a small segment of the golfing population carried risk but if it was done correctly, it could potentially revolutionize the way elite golf instruction is presented. Given John's youth and his intense motivation, he appeared to have a good shot at making his vision a reality.

John and I met in the winter of 1997 during his freshman year of high school. He had tried out for the St. Viator's golf team in the fall and been cut. In fact, he was the worst player at the tryouts by quite a bit. The coach told him, "You have no ability to play the game of golf and your best bet would be to choose another sport." Little did the coach know that before his career was over John would be a top-30 nationally ranked collegiate golfer.

In fairness to the coach, John as a high school freshman was downright bad. In that tryout, he shot between 120 and 140 for 18 holes. He had a great deal of room for improvement, in other words.

During our early conversations, I can remember him always being very engaged, not a common trait with junior golfers. He would ask insightful questions and constantly try to understand why a certain idea or technique either worked or didn't work. Other students simply wanted to hit the ball better, but that wasn't enough for John. He would stay around after his lessons, pounding ball after ball. The game was not natural to him, but he was resilient. I don't know many people, let alone kids, who can turn their high school coach's critical comments into pure motivation, but he could and he did. John was the kid who pushed himself to "Dig it out of the dirt," as Ben Hogan so famously said.

If done correctly, it could potentially revolutionize the way elite golf instruction is presented.

Working in the golf dome, we modified John's swing. By the time the snow melted, he had made some progress. We were getting him ready to compete in Illinois Junior Golf Association tournaments, the first one scheduled for late June. John played in that event and shot somewhere in the low- to mid-90s. From there, it was a summer of further dedication. By the end of the IJGA tournament season, he was scoring in the high 70s.

The very swift progress John made before sophomore year of high school became a base for him. He built off it to put together a solid career on the St. Viator team, quite unlikely given how it all started. However, when graduation came, it was a bleak time for him. Finding himself finished with high school and without any offers to play college golf was a shock to John. It devastated him emotionally.

A couple of months after graduation, I suggested he take a golf lesson from Dr. Jim Suttie. "Doc" was a legendary teacher around Chicago, one of the most respected golf instructors in the U.S. and a mentor to me. He was also the new coach at Florida Gulf Coast University. John was the first appointment in Doc's lesson book that day, the seven a.m. slot. When it was over, Doc told John he could practice as long as he wanted, having no idea how obsessive about practice the boy was. Some five hours later, John was still plugging away prompting Doc to wonder just how long the kid was going to tear up his range turf.

At seven p.m. that evening, Doc was done for the day and John was still pounding away. Impressed by this display of work ethic, Doc walked over and asked John where he was headed off to college. "Nowhere," John replied. "I wasn't recruited by anyone." Doc thought a moment. "Anyone who can hit that many golf balls in a single day can play for me," he said flatly. Somehow, in that one moment, all of John's hard work had paid off. He was a collegiate golfer. Doc Suttie had never in his life seen a happier kid.

John headed south to FGCU ecstatic to be a part of the team. Once he got there, he realized the other players on the team were better than he expected. To paraphrase Bobby Jones, John's new teammates were playing a game he was not familiar with. For an entire year, John finished at the bottom of the team during qualifying. Despite his every effort, he simply did not have the talent these kids possessed. Doc told John he had a lot of work to do over the summer. There would be new recruits coming in, and he was very much in jeopardy of not even making the team as a sophomore.

John responded in the only way he knew how—by digging it out of the dirt. For him, the summer between freshman and sophomore years was dedicated to endless 12-hour practice days, pounding ball after ball. Some days he continued past sundown into all hours of the night. His attention to detail was amazing. He was constantly writing down notes and goals in a black notebook he carried with him at all times. He sensed he was making progress, but even he couldn't have foreseen the breakthrough that was about to happen for him at the local U.S. Amateur qualifying event.

> Throughout the qualifier, John left his ego in the parking lot and deferred completely to his caddie's judgment.

One of his friends from junior golf, Ryan Cassidy, was at the time attending Indiana University and playing on the golf team there. Ryan was the guy to beat in Chicago and an AJGA All-American. I arranged for Ryan to be John's caddie at the qualifier, in large part because John knew Ryan had more tournament experience and more exposure to different types of championship courses. Throughout the qualifier, John left his ego in the parking lot and deferred completely to his caddie's judgment. They got in a groove where Ryan told John what to do on every shot, and John simply cleared his mind and trusted Ryan's judgment. Once the instructions on the shot were given to him, he would stand up to the ball and simply let it happen.

If John respects you and you know more about a particular subject than he does, he will go with your expertise as a specialist and not question it. John set a personal best of 68-70 to win the qualifier. He was headed to East Lake Country Club in Atlanta for the U.S. Amateur Championship. This achievement, startling on its own, was particularly important because he turned out to be the only member of his FGCU team to qualify. This was the moment John realized he no longer had to feel inferior to his teammates. He belonged.

That September, he was back on campus and with his game much improved. John's game wasn't always the prettiest but once his self-belief matched his work ethic, he started to break out. He ended up the year 29th in the nation in the Golfstat rankings, quite amazing for a kid who received not one single recruitment letter.

He'll also tell you that he started TPS because of the struggle he went through trying to find golf instruction geared toward accelerated learning.

Emboldened by this new level of success, and strongly influenced by the fact that his two best friends, Adam Gary and Derek Lamely (they were also the two most talented players on the team) were graduating, he decided to forego his final two years of college and turn professional.

His parents were incensed when John gave them the news. They were watching their son walk away from the chance to get his college degree—on scholarship, no less—while playing the sport he loved. John and his parents were so deeply divided by his decision that they did not speak to each other for many weeks. However, when his parents did break the silence it was to sit John down and have a conversation with him that would change his life.

They told him that, whether he realized it or not, he had a natural business mind and could succeed professionally no matter what field he tried. OK, pro golf would be first, but beyond that he needed a backup and they insisted he come up with one. The three of them sat down to discuss matters and what came out of it was a business plan. Adelle, John's mother, was experienced in writing them and as it turned out, John had an idea for a business already in his head. What they came up with at the end of that long afternoon was an outline of what the Player Service has, in fact, turned out to be.

John would be the first person to tell you that for a guy aiming to make a living playing golf, he had a number of significant holes in his game at the time he turned professional. In fact, it has to be said, and this is further testament to the dedication John exhibited, he simply did not possess legitimate PGA Tour talent.

Likely due to his amazing work ethic, he started out as a professional on a strong note. John actually won a few professional events in the early going. But by his own analysis, throughout those five years in the early 2000s when he was grinding on the mini-tour circuit, he didn't improve. In fact, he got steadily worse. His eventual assessment? He got worse as a pro due to the negative environment of the developmental tours along with poor training habits and technical, camera-based instruction. He'll also tell you that he started TPS because of the struggle he went through trying to find golf instruction geared toward accelerated learning for the competitive player, something he had desperately wanted and needed for himself.

His money ran out a few years into the tour-golf pursuit. As he would later state, he wasn't put on this earth to be a professional golfer.

John had come to the decision that his true calling was as a coach of young elite golfers. This became his inspiration and his sole goal. There was only one problem—no one would hire him. I suggested to John that he speak to some well-established head professionals and offer his services as a clubfitter as a way of getting his foot in the door. Although John will tell you he dislikes clubfitting, he is a natural at it and could have made an excellent living just doing that. He moved to Florida and approached Doc Suttie, his former college coach. John convinced Doc to hire him on a commission basis to handle the equipment needs of Doc's private students. John spent five months sleeping on an air mattress in a friend's apartment, fitting and selling clubs and absorbing everything he could from Dr. Jim Suttie on the training of high-level tour players.

The friend he stayed with was his former teammate at Florida Gulf Coast, Derek Lamely, whom John looked up to for his advanced playing ability. Derek had his PGA Tour card at the time and was doing his best to keep it. It was through Derek that John was able to obtain a Player's Coach badge, a credential that got him into any PGA Tour event on the schedule. These are the badges that tour players' swing coaches wear. John got his on Derek's say-so, even though he was not Derek's full-time swing coach. He was more a friendly face to help Derek feel more at home on the tour. John went to these tour events and just watched and studied, researching the coaching process on tour and shadowing the top instructors, Butch Harmon in particular. The coaching skill set he saw Butch exhibit with tour players was a thing unto itself in John's eyes.

In general, he came to recognize that tour players trained in a completely different way from the average serious player who is receiving traditional golf instruction. After enough time on the tour to decide that his own theory of golf performance training was sound, John returned to Chicago ready to test his training system. This was in 2010, the winter of my son Kyle's sophomore year in high school.

He came to recognize that tour players trained in a completely different way from the average serious player who is receiving traditional golf instruction.

Kyle's goal was to play top-echelon NCAA golf on scholarship at a Division 1 team. I had taught him how to play and helped him build his swing, which was mechanically very sound. Of course, there is more to golf than excellent mechanics, and I knew Kyle had a way to go in developing his training system and preparation habits.

Being in the business, I could have hired a number of reputable teachers for Kyle with way more experience and better resumes than John had. But knowing John and his journey, I felt that Kyle could learn a tremendous amount from him, both on and off the course. I had seen John's vision for coaching the elite player, and I knew his concepts were superior. In selecting a coach for my son, I wanted someone who thought outside the box, someone who wasn't afraid to have the tough conversations with him. As the results quickly showed, I had made the right choice.

He began to teach Kyle, and their work together produced extremely gratifying results. John's training system was amazing at taking something complex and simplifying it. In just one year, Kyle went from a very good local player to an All-American. John's personality and his unusual new training system were exactly what Kyle needed at the time.

Any of the three of us—John, Kyle or myself—could describe how John and Kyle went about working together as coach and player. But Kyle, as the student, is surely best equipped to do so in a meaningful way. He tells the story of their collaboration in the next chapter of this book.

Kyle Kochevar is the first student I ever worked with and I am forever grateful to him. I'm certain that without Kyle's belief and trust in my system, TPS would have never have come to fruition.

— J.P.

3
THE ART
OF
NEUTRALIZATION

2012 AJGA All-American
No. 1 Player in Illinois in 2012 Class
2014 Patriot All-American Champion
2018 PGA Tour China Member
2018 PGA Tour Canada Member
University of Virginia Graduate

Among all of us in TPS, I go back the farthest with John. As he says, I was his first student. I was also the first player he coached using the technique he calls "neutralization."

If someone asks what neutralization means, here's the simplest way to explain it: The ball flight creates the mechanics of the swing instead of the other way around.

Golf instruction is supposed to work best when it teaches a student to understand his or her swing well enough that they can coach themselves

KYLE KOCHEVAR

when necessary. The usual example is a player competing in a tournament and not hitting the ball solidly. They'll head straight to the range and try to come up with a new swing thought to fix the problem.

In that process, they are bound to think about mechanics. John understood how easily these experiments with mechanics can lead to even bigger problems, especially during competition. In my case, that was all the more possible due to my lack of interest in mechanics. I believe John devised his concept of neutralization with me because I simply don't relate to the mechanical facets of the swing or to the terminology that goes with all that. Possibly that's because I'm the son a golf instructor, and my dad taught me my swing so gradually that mechanical verbiage wasn't needed. I'm also left-handed, and I play golf left-handed. That is associated with being right-brain dominant, which I do feel I

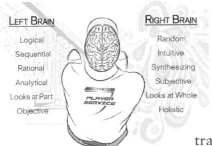

am. Being right-brain dominant, you will tend to be a lot more visual and intuitive and much less analytical.

Working with John and learning the technique of neutralization taught me to fix ball flight problems by going to the range and creating other ball flights. "Use one shot to fix another" is a phrase we use, which is another way to summarize the process. Neutralization has freed me up mentally and kept me away from paralysis by analysis.

We train in TPS using "periodization," which is the science of identifying ideal time periods to train your technical skills and ideal periods to train more by feel (one of my friends will talk about this in a later chapter). We're also taught in TPS that working on mechanics will always pull you out of the "flow state" or what most people call "the zone." If you're on the range using mechanical thoughts, you may feel like you're fixing things but, in my experience, it's nearly impossible to achieve peak performance when I'm being mechanical.

Pictures are the bridge from the conscious mind to the subconscious.

There are all sorts of problems that arise from the mechanical approach. It causes a golfer to operate in the left hemisphere of the brain and activates their pre-frontal cortex. You can't achieve your athletic potential that way. When a player achieves peak performance, or gets into the zone, they are in the right brain, more specifically, in the cerebellum. This is where the game feels effortless. You are living the present moment one shot at time, one moment at time.

When a player is mechanical or position-oriented, it causes them to be analytical and as a result, forces them to think with words instead of pictures. John's two favorite phrases are "Think with pictures, not words" and "Pictures are the bridge from the conscious mind to the subconscious."

Training with the neutralization concept allowed me to think with pictures and as a result, my game went to a whole new level.

From the beginning, I was coached by John to hit shallow cuts and fades, especially in practice. That was our way to control and offset my very pronounced draw and steep angle of attack. He and I began working together in 2009, when I was in 10th grade and looking ahead to my first season of American Junior Golf Association (AJGA) events. My dad, who had been my teacher up 'til then, was pulling back from that role as he had always planned to do. He wanted to hand me over to John because he and John have different coaching styles, and

John's system would get me to the next level. Going forward, it would be all about shooting a score, getting mentally tough for competition and learning to handle myself in tournament play, including the preparation. Sometimes your own father, even if he's an excellent swing instructor, isn't the right person for that job.

As the winter concluded, I became more and more immersed in neutralization. My dad would comment on how great my swing looked and that positions he and I had worked endlessly on were now so much sharper and more consistent. This blew my mind as I had not experienced a single conscious thought about positions.

Any time I was stuck on my swing or was having difficulty learning a new shot, John would just hit a shot and tell me to copy it. That makes it all the easier for a right-brained, left-handed golfer to pick up what they need by watching the coach "in the mirror." A phrase he often used was "See it. . .and do it." Never would he coach me so that I would see it, think about it, then try to do it.

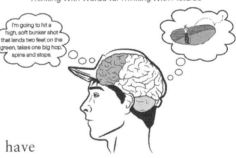

Performance of
Prefrontal Cortex vs. Cerebellum
Thinking With Words vs. Thinking With Pictures

I'm going to hit a high, soft bunker shot that lands two feet on the green, takes one big hop, spins and stops.

When the spring came, I was in a good place, feeling happy and feeling confident. John explained that we had achieved our goal. "You have all the shots now, Kyle," he told me. "You can work the ball either direction and control the trajectory. You now have the tools to play championship golf courses but more importantly, your training has engaged your right brain."

My first event in the spring was the AJGA event at Innisbrook in central Florida. John walked the cart paths watching me all the way. It was a 54-hole event with a cut after 36, and the field seemed stacked with talented players. At this point in my career, this was the biggest event I had ever played in. We agreed that I would play tee to green with a methodical feeling of targeting a zone and hitting to it—a positioning-type approach.

STAGES of CONSCIOUSNESS

Unconscious	Subconscious	Conscious
Information Assimilation	Information Sorting/Processing	Information Acquisition

SLEEPING	PLAYING	AWAKE
Theta-Delta Brainwaves	OPTIMAL PERFORMANCE Alpha Brainwaves	Beta Brainwaves

He and I also used music to help me get into a relaxed, confident zone, a state of mind where I was serious about winning the tournament, but still expecting to have fun in the process. He taught me that listening to music was a right-brain activity and as a result, would help me to get into the zone. I remember spending hours with him getting the playlist just right. John's attention to detail was amazing. At the time, I didn't realize how many things he taught me just by example. I find myself now, as an adult, very organized and detail-oriented.

Even par on the Copperhead course at Innisbrook is 71, which is what I shot on my final round. I finished in fifth place, losing to the likes of Daniel Berger and Patrick Rodgers. It was certainly my best round ever in a big, nationally-ranked tournament. I had no three-putts and no double-bogeys all week. The most important shot of the week came in the final round. It was a 6-iron from 175 yards to a tucked pin on a difficult par-4. The ball was a little below my feet in a fade lie, and that's what the shot called for. I executed the shot so well, I holed it; and remember, five months earlier I could hardly hit a cut or a fade if you gave me 10 chances. I walked up to the green to find my ball in the cup for eagle. What made me so proud of this moment was that I had a bunch of college coaches standing right behind me, and I had to hit a shot that was not natural to me. To pull it off the way I did really set the tone for me the rest of the year.

We came back from that Florida trip with momentum and as the season went on, we continued working. We stuck to the program that had worked—me hitting lots of fades and draws, using one ball flight to neutralize the extremes of the opposite ball flight. The next year, I played my final season for Glenbard West High School in Glen Ellyn, Illinois. By then, my national AJGA ranking was No. 15 in the U.S., and I had earned AJGA All-America status. Due to my tournament play, I was recruited by multiple Division 1 college programs. I decided on the University of Virginia, enrolling there as a freshman in the fall of 2012. It was truly a dream come true for me.

UVA is an amazing place to spend your college years with a very successful golf program. I was honored to become a Virginia Cavalier and represent the university as a member of the golf team. At the same time, it was definitely a change of pace for me with a different training system than what I was used to with TPS. I played well when I first got to college (by coincidence, our very first tournament was up in Chicago at Rich Harvest Farms). I finished middle-of-the-pack under difficult scoring conditions due to stormy weather.

Our team's next tournament was in Nashville. That didn't go well for me. My first round was pretty much a disaster, in terms of ball-striking. It was a blow to my confidence and it caused concern among the coaches, as well. They felt that swing changes were called for so I found myself going down the mechanical road. When I was practicing on my own, I would try to use my neutralizing technique, but slowly my mind shifted and I felt myself drifting into mechanical thoughts. This was to no fault of my coaches, as they have produced lots of quality players but for me, once I shifted into my left brain, I lost my secret weapon.

Due to my tournament play, I was recruited by multiple Division 1 college programs.

My better performances tended to come after I'd been home in Chicago and working with John. In the winter of my junior year, I made a trip home after a very disappointing semester in which I couldn't crack the lineup. John has a way about him that exudes confidence, which I needed. I came home feeling lost but after spending some time with him, I felt the old vibes coming back. I felt I had my swagger back. After some grinding on my golf game and lots of in-depth conversations on life, golf and mindsets, I went down to Arizona for an event called the Patriot All-American, which is one of the best amateur events in the world. John gave me one thought—*picture his swing.* I had gotten into a terrible tendency of coming over the top and hitting low pulls and wipe cuts. This picture worked well for me as John was an inside-out player who hit beautiful draws. I always loved his ball flight. As I made my way to Arizona, on every shot I just pictured his swing and ball flight.

I played those three rounds in a positive frame of mind, free of all technical thoughts, and shot 72-69-68. The deeper we got into the tournament, the better I felt. My ball-striking was spot on, my short game was really clicking and I began to get excited. Down the stretch, I was looking at the scores and thinking I could win the tournament outright. Well, almost. What happened instead is I got into a playoff with one other player. I remember standing on the tee as the playoff was about to begin, hearing John's voice in a whisper, telling me, "Think with pictures not words, Kyle." It was so clear and vivid it was almost as if he was there with me. I was able to stay in the zone, and beat my opponent on the second playoff hole with a great par on a difficult hole.

I can honestly say this was the biggest tournament win of my career. My journey has taught me so much, I kind of wish I could go back and tell myself as I was entering college, "Stick with what got you here." But as John always tells us, "Through adversity comes wisdom." I feel much wiser now.

TPS has been a second family to me. In a way, I feel like it all started with me. I am really proud to have been a part of it. Along the way, I have made lifetime friends and I believe TPS has helped me become a better version of myself. Obviously Innisbrook was a milestone for me, but it also was a big moment for TPS. It was where the program really got kick-started. And it turned out to be the place where John met the player who would become his second student, Brian Bullington. On that basis, it's only natural I hand the storytelling duties over to Brian.

Patriot All-America Video
https://www.youtube.com/watch?v=Ylubdl1jXGs

Brian Bullington's story shows that a little outside-the-box thinking can turn things around pretty quickly. You'll see what I mean by that as you read this chapter. My work with Brian grew directly out of the coaching I did with Kyle Kochevar. Brian was 16 when we began working together and, in hindsight, you could say he was the player that turned my original coaching practice into TPS.

— J.P.

4
THE TARGET IS MY *INTENTION*, NOT MY GOAL

BRIAN BULLINGTON

No. 1 Player in Illinois in 2011 Class
2013, 2014, 2015 All-Big Ten
2013, 2014, 2015 PING All-Region/Midwest
2016 and 2018 PGA Tour John Deere Classic Participant
2016 PGA Tour Latinoamérica Member
University of Iowa Graduate

Any time you're competing in a tournament, you don't want to have your head filled with distracting thoughts. That's a common belief among golf coaches and mental-side specialists. To keep that from happening, what do you do? Most people will tell you to block out all the negative or distracting thoughts "by focusing completely on the target." They believe that if you maximize target awareness, you can shield your mind from distractions.

I personally don't follow this advice. In years past—I'm currently 23, fresh off a playing career at the University of Iowa

and having recently turned professional—I did attempt to focus intently on my target. But the concept never worked for me. At this point, I wonder if it actually works for anybody. The target in golf isn't like the bullseye in archery or the catcher's mitt in baseball because golfers don't look at the target while they're executing their swing or their putting stroke. To John, this is an inherent contradiction, to be focused on something you can't even see during the athletic act you are undertaking. And that's just one of many flaws in the idea.

Of course, you need to conceptualize your intention in some way. You have to relate in some fashion to the target. We've found out that *awareness is different than intention.*

In working with John, and buying into his core concept about *focusing on what is controllable by me,* I've made significant progress as a competitor in the brief period of time since turning pro. As John likes to say, "The target represents 'try' and 'try' always creates tension." My attention is always on something I can actually control, even if that's a very subtle feeling about my tempo or my tension levels. "I'll take the golfer who is free over the ball and fearless when he makes his swing over the golfer who is trying to be target-aware." If you spend any time around John, you will hear him say that more than once.

Focus of attention is a part of your golf performance that John and I have worked on together for quite a while. His ideas about where you place your attention during your pre-shot routine are unique and have made a huge difference in my ability to play under pressure.

I turned professional in 2015 and started preparing for Q School. My goal was to make the Web.com Tour. I made it through first stage and felt very good about my chances. In first stage, I had shot under par and finished in the top 10. We played second-stage in Omaha, Nebraska at a golf course called ArborLinks. John travelled with me there, and we prepared by studying the course and talking about energy control. Once the competition started, I began to realize that second stage of Q School is not the same atmosphere as first stage. Everything feels more intense and significant. I got into a state where if I made a bogey, a lot of thoughts would race through my head about what that meant: Was I way outside the number? How would I feel if this didn't work out? In other words, all those ideas you get when you aren't in control of your process. I found myself focusing on things I couldn't control because I was making the target my goal. I was steering the ball and basically efforting my way along, trying to control each outcome.

I'll take the golfer who is free over the ball and fearless when he makes his swing over the golfer who is trying to be target aware.

As it turned out, I came up short and did not earn my Web.com Tour card. Afterward, John and I had a long and very productive talk about what had happened. The simple fact is that I was not ready physically or mentally to compete on that tour. This event became the turning point in my career. I was at rock bottom and ready to immerse myself fully in building a peak performance system. It's like the Buddhist saying, "When the student is ready, the teacher appears."

This was the moment when John gave me the most extensive

coaching I'd ever received. He and I developed a systematic mental approach broken into three steps—setting up the shot, creating my intention and then executing the intention. Each step had a detailed education course and an accountability step based on tracking key statistics. Two elements of this—first, where I placed my focus in creating my intention and then second, the execution phase—proved to be most valuable. John and I built a unique visual element to help me free up. Our shorthand for it was, "Make a field goal." He gave a football analogy that I really keyed into. What was particularly creative and unusual about using the uprights of a football goalpost as my visualization for golf shots is that I was allowed to "widen the distance between the two uprights" as much as I wanted.

Even more creative and unusual about the system was this: Visualizing the two goalpost uprights as a space my shot should pass through was not called "aiming" by John nor was I to think or feel that I was, indeed, "aiming" at the space between the uprights. By doing this, we took out any *conscious* or *active* wishing or wanting from the process of setting up to the shot and striking the shot. How does that work? It's simple: John would ask me: "Brian, do you want to hit the fairway?" "Do you want to hit the green?" "Do you want to make that putt?" Naturally my response would always be just to say "Yes." John would then say, "In that case, you don't have to try!"

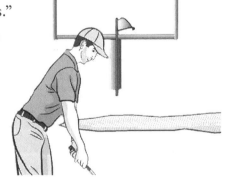

He would ask me, "Do you trust your instincts?" or perhaps, "Do you think great athletes trust their instincts when they're competing?" I would nod my head, and his next question would be along the lines of, "Do you think quarterbacks consciously aim before they throw the football?" "Do hockey players consciously aim when they shoot the puck? No, of course, they don't. They simply allow their instincts to take over and do the aiming for them." This concept really blew my mind, and once I just got out of the way and allowed my instincts to take over, my alignment became automatic. As a result, I felt at peace over the ball.

It's like the Buddhist saying, "When the student is ready, the teacher appears."

The next thing we worked on was finding my optimal performance state during the execution phase. We found that I'm actually in my optimal competitive state if it feels like I "don't care" in the conventional sense. As I worked with this mental concept, it proved itself to be a valuable tool over and over. The less I "cared," or was target-focused, the easier it was to hit excellent shots to the optimal positions on the golf course. Anyone who knows a little about the Buddhist concept of "No mind" will recognize the value of this technique in golf. After I've imagined the goalpost and the uprights in a desired configuration between me and the ideal position where the shot should end up, I get into the address position. I have a subtle sense with my peripheral vision of where the ball will fly but basically, I have no thoughts in my head. I am thinking of nothing.

If you've read this far, you can probably see that John believes training for golf should resemble the training people undergo to refine their athletic motion in sports like basketball, hockey and baseball. As he worked with us, and worked on his concepts, John would be thinking all the time about how different he felt on a basketball court or a baseball diamond versus out on the golf course.

As he explains it to us, the core of it all is athletic reaction. A basketball hits off the back of the rim, you catch it, take one dribble to get free and put up a six-foot shot that goes in for two points. In the few seconds it takes for that to happen, there are multiple athletic acts, but there is basically no thinking—it's all reaction. There isn't any "wanting" with regard to the shot going in or the two points going up on the scoreboard. The basketball player who makes this play doesn't feel like he is making decisions, or that he is aiming the ball at the hoop or backboard. So, there is a freedom to everything he does.

> I've been able to test this system over the last several months, and the results have been pretty amazing.

What John said to me about hitting shots in golf tournaments is this, "Let's create a way to make it a reaction." Obviously, as golfers, we can experience that no-aim, no-thought, no-effort, not-caring sensation, but it's almost always when we're practicing and just happen to feel totally relaxed over a pitch shot or a long putt, and we knock it in. John told me we could extend that to competition. He said that as long as I fully executed the TPS training system in my preparation and I chose to trust my new mental approach, my game would hold up in any type of pressure situation even on the 72nd hole of the U.S Open.

I have been able to test this system over the last several months, and the results have been pretty amazing. In February, I was able to earn my PGA Tour Latinoamérica card. In addition, my new-found mindset helped me to Monday-qualify for a Web.com Tour event (the Rust-Oleum Championship, at the Ivanhoe Club outside Chicago). I also made my first PGA Tour start at the John Deere Classic.

Belonging to TPS has surrounded me with players who, in total, are better than I am. But that's true of all of us. It's even true of whomever happens to be playing the best and winning the most at a given time. Within the group, there will always be a better wedge player or a better mid-iron player, a longer driver, a more accurate driver, a better bunker player—all those skills, except the one in which you, yourself, might happen to excel. We're all friends. The success of one TPS player doesn't make me envious. It makes me hungry to match what they've done or even do better than what they've done. Improvement, reaching new goals, that becomes contagious at TPS.

It's especially good to be surrounded by players like that when we've got John at the center of things, coaching us all and making sure our good energy keeps flowing. There is something about youth sports, or maybe it's junior golf, that makes it very unusual to hear honest assessments from the adults. If you spend a lot of time in the competitive junior golf environment, you'll hear John speak and he will sound blunt. He lacks the ability to sound sincere when he's saying something he doesn't mean, so he doesn't even try. He will watch me hitting shots on the range or working on short game and he will say straight out, "That's just not going to get it done." But as he says something like that, you know that his mind is working on how he needs to coach you to address the particular problem. It's always said out of passion for bringing out our potential.

As players, we have great camaraderie, we care about each other, but our reason for being here is simple: We are trying to get better. As good a coach as John is—the best in the business, we all feel—he is constantly trying to improve, too. My good friend Charlie Netzel will take it from here. He'll dive deeper into the visualization skills necessary to clearly create your intention!

Training at TPS tends to be challenging for students, at least in the beginning. That's because many of our core concepts are generally unfamiliar—plenty of them go against accepted beliefs we're all familiar with. Charlie's case offers clear evidence that an open mind to simple concepts can pay huge dividends.

— J.P.

5
REAL TIME
VISUALIZATION

CHARLIE NETZEL

No. 1 Player in Illinois in 2013 Class
2014 and 2017 Colleton River Intercollegiate Champion
2016 and 2017 Srixon/Cleveland Scholar
2017 All-Big Ten Golfer
2018 PGA Tour China Member
Michigan State Graduate

Even before the Player Service was officially a company, there were five or six
of us working with John and getting
exposed to his ideas. He was developing
and refining a lot of new concepts at the
time. They were unlike the golf-instruc-
tion approaches we were used to.

The first unusual feature of working
with John was that he gathered us in a
group as often as possible. Growing up,
we had been told that elite golf instruction
is one-on-one—all about private lessons.
But we would never raise that point to
him because we loved the way it felt to be

working together in our group. We were excited to be developing great friendships and rivalries. We competed hard against each other but, at the same time, we cared about each other.

John understood that. He firmly believed that forming these bonds would make us better people in the long run. He remembered how the team sports he had played fostered so many close friendships. The personal relationships, in his view, would increase each player's intensity and inspire us as athletes to put our hearts into practicing and getting better. In golf, a junior who is always one-on-one with a coach can get apathetic, usually without realizing it. They wind up going through the motions. We've all known players who ended up like that. Meanwhile, when your junior-golf years are over and you're headed off to college and adult life, every good friendship you've ever formed ends up contributing to your maturity.

> If you want to improve, John wants to help you and he'll find a way to do it.

As I prepare for my senior year at Michigan State University, I find myself looking back and realizing that John, as a young teacher, actually needed a group around him. If he had worked one-on-one only, he would not have become the coach he is today. His eye is super-sharp; it catches everything that happens. Also, his mind works phenomenally quickly. John has a very active almost restless mind when it comes to golf performance. As he implements new approaches, he needs a lot of real-time feedback. The TPS group gives him that. Plus, he feeds off our camaraderie.

If you want to improve, John wants to help you, and he will find a way to do it. Along the way, you will develop a personal relationship with him that's extremely valuable to both coach and student. He noticed that the way I like to move around the golf course and position myself was a lot like his own style as a player. Our temperaments are different. He was outwardly intense and demonstrative while I'm more cool and even-tempered, but we're similar strategically as players. We also have other traits in common, for example, being fastidious about our clubs. If I see dirt in the grooves of somebody's irons, I shake my head, and John's the same way. He will watch an iron shot in flight and he'll be able to tell that it came off a clubface with dirty grooves, which to him is inexcusable.

When he's speaking directly to you, it's like you're the only person in the world. He has a tremendous accumulation of knowledge about each of his individual students, and while he is coaching you, his mind is scanning through all those details and observations. The usual result is that he'll hit upon the concept that will work best for you in that moment.

When he isn't focused on one student, his mind is churning along, making all these little discoveries. It's as though all the things that have ever been said or written about the golf swing or shotmaking or scoring are streaming through his thoughts, and he's challenging these conventional beliefs by holding them up against what he sees in his own students. Of course, it helps that we have all different body types and swings and personalities because that diversity tests the value of any performance concept much more stringently.

As a TPS student, you get used to the way John will move through the group, watching his players and saying all these interesting things about what various students are trying to do and what it takes to improve at the different facets of the game. You'll hear him make a statement and it will sound pretty smart, but it won't actually seem useful to you. Then a half-minute later, he'll say something else and—same thing—it's interesting but you forget it pretty quickly.

Then he'll say something that makes you stop everything you're doing. It will be this amazing truth and you will know right then there's no way you won't think about what he has just said 100 times or more, and you'll probably never forget it. Yet, for the player right next to you, it will barely register. It's the same way for things he says that don't click with you—they will end up being highly important to the next student down the line.

What was ultimately so helpful about this dynamic is the freedom it provided. It showed me that many fine ideas about hitting golf shots and playing competitive rounds don't deserve much attention from me. They're all well and good, but they don't happen to be my own best triggers for striking the ball or getting it in the hole. They're someone else's good triggers. That's a very liberating thought in a sport that sends so much information at you and gives you so much time to ponder it.

I started in John's program in my sophomore year in high school and every year I was with him, I got better. One day in mid-May of my senior year, John had us gathered at Oak Brook Golf Club, a public course west of Chicago where we often practiced. He was giving us a new concept for our pre-shot preparation and the pre-shot routine. Up until then, I had been a decent competitive junior and a decent player on my high school team. After that day, I found I was a different golfer—dramatically improved and able to hold my own against strong competition on any given day.

What he told us was both simple and brilliant: "To hit a great shot, you have to have a crystal clear intention." To get that type of clarity, you needed to develop a skill called *real-time visualization*. He told us this was essential to what he called "full engagement," or getting the clear, entire picture of the swing, the stroke and the shot in full flight.

The first step was to go through our pre-shot routine, many times over, speaking out loud what we normally kept as silent thoughts, and do this to a constant metronome beat *with John and all the other players listening.*

To hit a great shot, you have to have a crystal clear intention.

Up until that day, I had never done such a thing. I would never have thought to state my intention out loud. I'm sure none of us had. Once the session got going, and players were audibly stating the steps to their pre-shot routine, I found the experience to be strange. A non-golfer may not understand this, but to speak your inner thoughts as you're getting ready to hit a shot takes something that's very private and really puts it out there. The longer we did this, however, the less I found it to be weird and the more I found it enjoyable. The key to the exercise was the application of the metronome. John would always say that the purpose of the pre-shot routine was to quiet your mind and create the rhythm that you needed to execute your best swing. And the beat of the metronome was a big support for that process.

There was another activity John gave to us, similar in nature. It took something we kept private and brought it into the open, and this served to bring us together as a group at the same time that it provided a lot of insights. Through this activity, we learned that one player in the group routinely shut their eyes for two seconds to get calm, and that someone else pulled on the brim of their cap as a sign to themselves that they had committed to the shot. Everyone's thoughts and quirks would trigger the next person to reveal what they did. To me, this form of sharing was just another great thing about being part of TPS.

In these exercises, you could recognize where another player was getting into specific detail, but also where they were fuzzy in their attention or totally skipped over something important. Then, when it was your turn again, you saw exactly what your own technique for the pre-shot lacked. You could see the parts that were consistent and the parts that weren't. To this day, I use this technique in a slightly modified way. I refer to it as "Say the shot, then hit the shot."

This is a digression, but one night about a year later, I was at my desk reading over a three-page paper I had written and would be handing in the next day. I gave it some final edits and then decided to read it out loud, the way they teach you in expository writing. As I was doing so, I remembered the day John first taught us real-time visualization. It hit me that reading a paper out loud and doing your pre-shot out loud are very similar. In both cases, you are moving to a more refined level of awareness. You're seeing more, you're recognizing things more clearly, and it all feels more urgent and significant.

With our pre-shot patterns significantly sharpened, John's next step for us was to actually see the shot *for the full duration it took to complete.* For me this was especially important to my pace and speed on the putting green. In the past, I would form a mental picture of the ball going in the hole—nothing more than that. John explained that real-time visualization is in fact visualizing the pace at which the ball needs to roll to make the putt drop. He took this concept to the point where he would pull out a stopwatch and time how many seconds a putt needed to reach the hole, and then challenge us to visualize the ball rolling for that exact amount of time. On shorter putts, he would have us visualize how many revolutions the ball would make before it drops.

"Say the shot, then hit the shot."

This concept opened my eyes to many related concepts. One that blew my mind was the fact that downhill putts roll slower and take more time to reach the cup than uphill putts. Another was that, on fast greens, the ball rolls slowly, whereas on slow greens it travels quickly. These seem like paradoxes, but as you experiment you see that it all makes total sense. I was able to internalize the fact that on downhill putts, I would need to hit the putt more lightly and let gravity take over to roll my ball to the hole. Conversely, uphill putts would require more energy and would start off rolling fast, then rather suddenly lose steam as the slope acted upon the ball, almost like velcro. Once I wrapped my brain around this, my speed on the greens became automatic. I became adept at visualizing the roll of the ball—its initial pace, where it would turn, how far it would roll out and so forth. All these dynamics became more specific and refined.

John would emphasize to us that *visualization connects our conscious mind to our subconscious mind* and that peak performance only occurs w*hen the subconscious mind is dominant.* In golf, we need highly advanced visualization skills. You know you've got them when you produce the shot you planned and it never feels like a surprise. John has often mentioned that when a player is using real-time visualization to its maximum potential, once they are over the ball, they'll get a strange sense of déjà vu. They will feel as though they have already hit the shot.

In his view, visualization is at the core of mental training because it's the bridge from the left brain to the right brain. TPS players are trained to understand that the brain is more efficient and effective when you are seeing pictures rather than thinking in words. We are told that, if you can combine this fundamental with optimal focus of attention, your mental game will hold up under extremely intense pressure.

As I said, this piece of coaching from John produced a true breakthrough in my golf game. Later that same month, I played a 36-hole Illinois Junior Golf Association event at Medinah Country Club—on the iconic No. 3 Course there—and put together a bogey-free, 5-under round on the first day. I came back the next day and played solid golf using this real-time visualization technique on every shot. I was able to win the event by seven strokes.

A week later, I had another IJGA win, in the DuPage Junior World Qualifier at Maple Meadows. Again, it was a 36-hole tournament and again I won by seven strokes. The top three finishers in that event qualify to play in the Junior World Championship. As I said, I was nearing the end of my junior career never having stood out from the crowd. Thanks to what I discovered on that day John taught us real-time visualization, I went on a tear the rest of the season, winning several more times, including my first AJGA title. I ended up the No. 1 junior in the state of Illinois, and ranked in the top 80 in the entire U.S. It's pretty amazing for any player to break out in this manner without making even the slightest swing change.

To this day I use the real-time visualization technique on-course. Even on the practice tee, I will often be visualizing a drill or a swing thought. I find it very powerful to be able to visualize the various parts of my swing motion. For me to perform at my best, I can't be thinking about mechanics one bit. Visualizing the ball as it is launching and dropping toward the target really helps me get in the right mindset and attain my optimal performance state. Because of how "pure" this type of visualization can be, it will also have the effect of quieting my mind. It brought a noticeable consistency to the tempo of my pre-shot movements when I was first incorporating it. I was getting up to the ball, looking at the shot, visualizing ball flight, pulling a club and striking the shot in a particular tempo that was repeating itself. I'm happy to say, that has continued.

To be a great coach you have to be one of those people who believes that we as humans have a ton of potential that we will never realize unless we push past our barriers. It won't happen if we just do what everyone else does. John is certainly that kind of person, which is probably a blessing and a curse for any top-tier coach: You see the amazing things people could accomplish, but then you see how disappointingly short everyone falls of what is actually possible for them.

Obviously, golf performance is filled with ups and downs, and John's ability to be creative when a player is in a funk is remarkable. For example, in my freshman year at Michigan State University, I was in a funk. John gave me an assignment on my plane ride down to a tournament in South Carolina. He suggested I close my eyes, quiet my mind and ask myself, "What are the 10 reasons I should win this tournament?" Once I had my 10 reasons identified, I was to take a sheet of paper and carefully write them down. Then when we landed and arrived at the gate, I was to walk off the plane and throw the piece of paper in the trash.

While going through this exercise, I started to see myself winning the event. I saw my swing moving freely and effortlessly. I could see putts tracking to the cup and falling in. The experience became so vivid I could even hear the sound of purely struck shots, and I could hear my ball actually dropping in the hole. It became almost an out-of-body experience in which I was physically sitting on a plane even as my mind was 30,000 feet below, playing the golf course. John later explained this phenomenon to me. He said I had reached a deeper level of real-time visualization, and that I was only able to reach it because of all the visualization training I had done earlier in my career.

This was yet another example of John's unconventional coaching tactics. My "10 Reasons" process helped build my confidence and give me the vision and belief that I had the game to win. At the same time, throwing the paper away as I walked off the plane symbolized that these thoughts weren't going to be useful to me while playing. While competing, I would need to focus on being in the present moment and on my real-time visualization. Once I walked into that airport terminal, a strong sense of calm and confidence came over me. When I got to the golf course, my pictures were clear and I truly believed I could win.

No.	Month	Day	Year
14	March 8, 2014		

10 Reasons Why I'm Going to Win

☑	1.	I have accomplished my practice goals every day since my last event.
☑	2.	I have done all the little things to prepare for the event.
☑	3.	I have the support of my family, friends and coaches.
☑	4.	I am going to stay in the present for the entire event.
☑	5.	I have executed the TPS neutralizing system.
☑	6.	I have reached all my TPS combined goals.
☑	7.	I believe in myself, as do my coaches and family.
☑	8.	I have embraced the mentality that mindset beats skillset.
☑	9.	I am going to make aggressive swings at conservative targets.
☑	10.	I will not let the outcome of my shots determine my emotion.

And in fact, I did win. The tournament—by coincidence it was hosted by Michigan State, my own school—was the Colleton River Collegiate, a 54-hole event on two golf courses. I shot 78-68-70 to end up co-medalist, then won a two-man playoff to take the individual title. It was amazing to me how at the trophy presentation, a powerful sense of déjà vu came over me. There was no way I could feel surprised at that outcome because in my mind, the tournament had already been played, and I had already won.

My former high school teammate, Dan Hudson, will take it from here and explain how our training cycles work to maximize our performance in the biggest events.

Visualization Video
https://www.youtube.com/watch?v=efJy0zm0uec&t=2s

Dan Hudson possesses a tenacious work ethic and extreme discipline. He is the player who most emphatically has shown his peers in TPS what hard work looks like. Dan is an amazing player. That being said, because he exhibits so many attributes of high achievers, I am certain Dan will be successful at anything he tackles in life.

— J.P.

6
THE ADVANTAGE
OF
PERIODIZATION

DAN HUDSON

2015 and 2016 Academic All-Big 12 Team
2017 All-Big 12 Tournament Team
2017 and 2018 Academic All-American
Top 10 in Kansas Jayhawk Career Scoring
2018 PGA Tour Canada Member
University of Kansas Graduate

Every junior golfer who trains with TPS commits to a year-long contract. That's a good thing for the player and it's a good thing for our group because it provides continuity. It also creates a feeling that we're pushing each other to improve and we're developing our skills together.

Over the course of a year, we use a training pattern called "periodization," which is used by many Olympic athletes, as well. With periodization, your year is divided into segments and you devote each calendar segment to a particular style of training, whether it be physical training, technique and skill acquisition, mental training or peak-performance work. TPS students start out in November devoting 90% of training time to golf swing and putting mechanics in combination with our work on clubhead speed acquisition. By the time spring arrives, we are splitting our time 50-50 between fitness/technique and mental skills/course management for scoring and competitive performance.

Eventually, as the tournament season is set to begin, we are in a 90-10 split, 90% of our time devoted to on-course performance plus some specific skill acquisition, and just 10% on mechanics and full-swing technique. In the month of July, our TPS training center hosts a lot of college golf coaches, so that's another important segment of the year for which we get special preparation.

The TPS version of periodization means that if your swing isn't in good form coming into the tournament season, you don't try to take it apart and put it back together. Instead you focus on "owning" your current motion and using course strategy and self-management to navigate the golf course. Once we've reached the 50-50 split period, we're told to "Max out your performance with what you have." John set it up this way partly to keep us motivated during the months when we're not playing tournaments. In addition, he believes mechanical thoughts will pull us out of the optimal-performance state of mind. As each competitive season ends, we all understand what our technical swing issues might be, and we'll address them without

PERIODIZATION

Technical
&
Physical
90%
70%
30%
10%
Mental
&
Strategic

10%
30%
70%
90%

delay knowing there's a limited window for working on mechanics.

Once a TPS golfer heads off to college, the periodization time splits change, and each calendar year will have two cycles instead of one. This is to account for the fact that we play tournaments in fall and spring rather than in the summertime, as you do in junior golf.

Max out your performance with what you have.

In my case, when all the recruitment activity was over, I ended up committing to play at the University of Kansas as a member of the Jayhawk men's golf team. I struggled there in the very early going, but have played steadily better golf as I've made adjustments and gained experience. You'll hear over and over that the transition from high school to college is a challenge. In my opinion, it is particularly hard for a golfer. You swap one very detailed routine for a much different one and however much you liked the old routine, it doesn't matter. You just have to go with the flow. At that point, you will realize how stuck in your ways you can be even as a teenager.

When John started coaching juniors back in 2010, he had an original core of a half-dozen players. He was training them at the same time that he was tweaking and finalizing the structure of his system. I was one of the first players to come in behind that first group. I got interested in TPS because I was friends with Charlie Netzel, one of the players in John's original group. Charlie and I went to Lyons Township High together, and I had a close-up view of his golf game. I saw it undergo a dramatic improvement based on his work with this new coach, John Perna.

Initially after speaking with John, I set up a trial period so I could assess over the course of a few months whether his system seemed likely to work well for me. I realized right away that John was more than just a guy who gives swing tips in a Saturday-morning lesson, he was deeply serious about providing us everything we needed to succeed in competition.

Be solution-oriented, not problem-driven.

I only worked with him a short while before the two of us sat down and set up some goals for me. At that point, he explained periodization. There's a powerful belief in the value of all these training segments within TPS. When you're in the early parts of the year, you bring a work ethic where you treat the day's practice session as if it's the last one of your life. You give it everything. But when the tournaments come along, you need a new attitude: Competition has to be fun and you have to jump in with a fearless attitude. The idea is to lace up your spikes and let it happen. At that point, you're relying on your gut more than your head. You're using intuition and instinct instead of relying on the mind's typical way of thinking. "Allow your body to do what your mind sees" is our concept. The "allowing" part is what's challenging. Personally, I have taken longer than some other players to get in sync with that but over time, I've been able to do it more and more.

As I mentioned, freshman year at Kansas was a difficult period for me. In the summer before heading off to school, my game was in excellent shape. I competed in the U.S. Amateur at Atlanta Athletic Club, striking the ball very well and missing match play by a single stroke. A few weeks later, I was at KU and wondering what happened to my golf game. The coaches set up a six-round team qualifier and out of 12 Kansas players, I finished dead last by 10 shots. Needless to say, I didn't compete in our first tournament. I did get into the next two tournaments but didn't play well. After that, I went through the rest of the fall not playing in our tournaments.

When the semester was over, John and I sat down with the attitude of "let's-figure-this-out." One of John's trademark sayings is "Be solution-oriented, not problem-driven." He told me we should start with statistics. We needed to look at my play and my scoring objectively based on the numbers. What stood out from the score analysis was how poorly I had scored on par-5 holes. We isolated the problem of way below-average driving accuracy. I was putting myself in a position where I couldn't attack. From where my drives were ending up, the idea of making birdie, much less eagle, wasn't even a consideration. So we had something we could work with, something "measurable," to use a word you'll hear a lot in TPS training.

Since we were heading into the competition portion of our periodization training, and we were not going to be able to focus on mechanics, John decided an equipment change was needed. We went to his club builder and had him make me up a driver with a cut tendency and 3-wood with fairly similar loft but with a center of mass that set up a draw tendency. "We're going to build your bag off the par-5s" is how John put it. He made me vow never to use the driver on a hole that demanded a right-to-left shot off the tee, and never to use the 3-wood on a hole that demanded left-to-right trajectory off the tee. I was also to use the 3-wood off a tee only, never off the deck.

We worked with these clubs until I had confidence in the new plan; meanwhile we did some other skill-based, short-game training. Then it was time for me to head back down to Kansas for second semester. The results were good. I went from only hitting 44% of the fairways and playing the par 5s over par to hitting 72% of the fairways and playing the par 5s at almost a half-shot under par. That spring I played in every one of our team tournaments and I was never outside the top 25 in any of them, with a couple of top-10 finishes in there as well. From being a complete bust in the fall season, I had become one of the top players on our team in the spring tournaments.

In hindsight, I understand what happened to me at the beginning of freshman year. In my time at TPS, we had built a training system where if I executed the plan, it was inevitable that I would play well. Then I left home, left TPS and I was in a different system, one that used a different schedule and different techniques. That was the program, and I was having trouble getting with the program. I would be participating in team practices thinking, "Why don't I have the option to do my TPS System?" I got frustrated mentally. It was a bit of immaturity on my part. The plain fact is, when you enter a system, you have to adapt to it. That's just reality. I got home at Christmas break and regrouped. John and I talked things over, we built those new clubs for me, he gave me a couple of drills and we agreed that whatever the results, good or bad, I would stick with our new streamlined plan. And as I said, things got a lot better.

The more you experience college golf, the more you understand that a four-year NCAA golf career is going to contain a little bit of everything. At KU, my turning point came at a tournament down in Mississippi in the pouring rain on a day when my golf swing was not working at all, especially with the driver. It's one thing to play in wretched weather conditions, but to be spraying the ball all over the place at the same time is double the misery. My coach came out to see me early in the round, and I had to tell him I had no idea where the ball was going. One hole, I would slice my tee shot off the planet, so the next hole I'd aim way left, then double-cross myself with a huge hook.

After I finished talking to my coach, I hit an iron shot into a deep greenside bunker but managed to get up and down for a great par. The next hole, I blew one into the woods, found the ball then punched a low shot through about 100 yards of trees, which set up another par. My coach hung with our group and I kept hitting into trouble and somehow escaping.

After the round, he said he was thinking about finding me an orange hunting vest given how deep into the woods I was having to walk. But he also said that my round of golf that day was one of the most impressive displays of determination he had ever seen.

In my time at TPS, we had built a training system where, if I executed the plan, it was inevitable that I would play well.

What's strange is that I had spent a good portion of my junior-golf career losing to players who would patch together a decent score in this manner. I was the type of kid who loved standing on the range hitting balls for hours. I wasn't that interested in short-game play, so I'd lose strokes around the green and get beaten by players who could get it in the hole even with tee-to-green play that was mediocre or worse. In my eyes, the reason for my newfound scoring success was having trust in the training plan John and I laid out at semester break and sticking to it. TPS periodization training really emphasizes short-game work during the competition cycle. Looking back, I can see that when I stopped thinking about my swing and ball-striking, it freed up much more time for me to put into short-game training.

I was also doing a better job on the mental side of the game. A big part of that was becoming solution-oriented. I began enjoying the challenge of shooting as low as possible on days when I didn't have my "A" game. Putting in the hours and putting in the effort has never been a problem for me, no matter what part of TPS training we're talking about. John would look at me and say, "Dan, you've done everything in the system. Everything you've been asked to do, you've done. Just get over the ball and let it go." John is rightly proud of how unique and comprehensive his system is. As I said earlier, there is basically no way for me not to play well if I execute it. So he builds my confidence by telling me all the time how complete my training has been, and how much I've put into my preparation. Logically, I can't argue with that.

So whenever John has a new drill he wants to introduce or a new wrinkle he's planning to add to his business model, he will call me and ask my opinion, and we'll talk frankly about the pros and cons of whatever it is. In that sense, we have something more than a coach-athlete relationship. In fact, if you asked me to name my five best friends, John would be one of them. We talk at least once a week and well over 50% of the time it has nothing to do with golf. With John, the conversation will wander around, but underneath nearly everything he says is one core message—he believes in me. As he talks, he doesn't seem to be giving a motivational speech, but every time our conversation ends, I come away motivated. I'm ready to put everything I've got into whatever it is I need to do next.

I have complete belief in him as a coach but at the same time, he and I are constantly debating and disagreeing on subjects of all kinds. And yet, it's always constructive. We love to get into debates with each other and I think that's because our minds work the same way. We're both very analytical, but we try to bring all the creativity we can to the process of figuring things out and problem solving.

One example in particular stands out. Early in my days at TPS, John was refining his course-management system, which would become a huge asset to his students. He was doing extensive research on tour players and their dispersion patterns and how they attack golf courses. Out of that came a new approach based on percentages—a system for knowing where to aim and how to take hazards out of play. It's a cumulative thing because we use feedback to assess our ability to execute it without looking at conventional stats like fairways and greens and putts. It was amazing how detailed it was, but what I found very cool was he listened to our input and authentically cared about our thoughts and concerns.

I consider it unusual that a coach as accomplished as John would be open-minded to what a bunch of high school kids thought of his concepts. It was an experience I recall very often, being at such an early stage of life and finding out my opinion mattered. Interactions like that have, over our time in TPS, instilled self-confidence in all of us. As I look back now, I'm not so sure John really needed our opinion, but I think he knew what it meant to us that we thought he did!

Thanks for taking some time to find out about my experience in TPS. From here, my longtime training partner, Robert Renner, will dive into the swing-building phase of periodization.

Robert Renner is a freak athlete and a wonderful kid. He came late to golf after long years of devotion to youth hockey. I can say with a lot of confidence that without our unique training concept for developing mechanics, Robert would not have reached his potential so quickly. He was the first player to show us the immense value of building sound swing mechanics with little or no conscious mechanical thoughts.

— J.P.

7
BUILDING A BIOMECHANICALLY SOUND SWING
(without thinking about mechanics)

2012 and 2013 CDGA Illinois State Junior Champion
2013 All-State Hockey Player and Golfer
Florida Gulf Coast University Graduate

Junior golfers who come through TPS are encouraged to genuinely enjoy tournament competition, to remember we're supposed to have fun out there. We're also taught to employ a strategy based on limiting the risk of each shot as we plan it out, then executing our shots in an aggressive, even fearless style.

It should have been easy for me, as a former hockey player, to adopt this competitive approach, or so you'd think. In fact, it was the opposite. My training in hockey started before kindergarten so by the time I switched to golf in high school my body was completely wired for reaction, reflex and response. In hockey, the action seems to occur in

ROBERT RENNER

split-seconds. In golf, the ball is sitting there and you've got all the time in the world to look around at the rough, the trees and the various hazards. Of all the TPS students John worked with in the early years, I was the one most paralyzed by overthinking. And so I became the one who pushed John to devise as many methods as possible for countering this problem in a player.

> You need to be happy out there or you won't ever get in the zone of top performance.

John relates very well with someone like me based on my athleticism as a high-level player in a team sport. Playing several team sports was a big part of John's life as he was growing up. The divergence in the general training styles between hockey and golf caused problems for me, but all John ever told me about playing hockey was that it would help my golf in a big way. This was good for me to hear. One thing about our coach—he knows how the human mind works. I would say he has a true genius for that. I eventually came to realize that a lot of the instruction John gives me has nothing to do with mechanics. The purpose of it is to harmlessly distract me from being too analytical about my swing.

John also carries over to golf that team sport atmosphere where players are permitted to give each other the needle. TPS kids are allowed to give each other grief, as long as we do it in the right way. John's students, even though we put all our trust in him, also give John a lot of razzing, and he's fine with that. I don't think he'd be comfortable if we didn't bust his chops now and then. He likes the energy of the group when things are loose and you can feel the undercurrent of our rivalries. It helps keep all of us humble, including him.

John would constantly remind us that golf is just a game. You need to be happy out there or you won't ever get in the zone of top performance. I remember from my hockey years the scrimmages where we would be chirping at each other and talking some trash. That's when our skating was at its best, it's when our passing and shooting was at its sharpest and quickest. I've been on teams that got into that kind of groove in practice and then, when a big tournament came along, would switch to a grim and serious attitude with very poor results.

I went to the same high school as John, St. Viator. When I got serious about golf, I had just enough ability, plus some experience in a few junior tournaments, to look like a reasonable No. 6 player on the high school team. The St. Viator coach, who had been John's coach, sent me to him with the idea I might become a No. 6 player who could maybe do a little more than simply fill out the squad. But John saw more in me and by the time it was all over, his instincts were proven right. As a senior, I set a school record winning six of our eight invitational tournaments, which was a pretty big accomplishment for a guy slotted to be the No. 6 player.

> John is rightly proud of how unique and comprehensive his system is. As I said earlier, there is basically no way for me not to play well if I execute it.

A lot of my work in TPS has been about speed from two different perspectives. One involves my pace in the pre-shot routine and in hitting shots during competition. The other involves generating raw clubhead speed. I think my improvement happened so quickly because John associated so much of what I had to do in golf with what I had already done in hockey.

When I was struggling with my routine and mental process, he coached me to think of striking a golf ball as the equivalent of a "one-timer" in hockey. For any non-fans reading this, that's a slap shot on a puck that is sliding toward you. You don't do any stick work to position the puck, you just shoot it. In general, the message of don't-think-just-react (once a golf shot has been strategized and planned out) has been heard many times by me during my TPS training. Finally accepting that part of the teaching was a huge mental breakthrough for me.

The evolution of my swing was pretty amazing. No one was more amazed than I was. What particularly stood out was how much clubhead speed I was able to gain after joining TPS. We never touched weights; we never stepped foot in the gym. Nor did John take my swing apart. I really never thought about my swing or had to try and manipulate it into any particular positions. John designed a "clubhead-speed system" based on a series of drills focusing on ground-force reaction, proper pivot, hand speed and body-arm sequence. We trained all winter as a group and followed a specific curriculum that he created. By the end of that winter, we had all gained tons of speed and were hitting the ball much more solidly. If you want the "measurable," my clubhead speed with the driver went from 108 mph up to 124 mph. I actually had to get used to the explosive feeling of impact. I was smashing the ball in a way I had never experienced.

In the TPS speed training system, velocity and stability are two goals you work toward simultaneously. One exercise that really helped my swing was the separation drill. You stand on a wobble board holding a club and pressing a ball between your legs. On the way back, you try to separate your center of pressure from your center of mass while moving pressure into your trail heel, which gives you the sensation of creating coil. From that position at the top, you start your move down and your lower body shifts your pressure forward on the wobble board while you simultaneously rotate your lead hip and knee. The move will cause your legs to squat. This results in your knees separating and the ball dropping. From there, you just smash through the golf ball with a feeling of effortless power.

Another favorite of mine was our "over-speed" training protocol, where we take ropes, chains and shafts of differing weights and flexes and generate as much speed as we can. The concept behind it is very cool and empowering. A lot of instructors will stand there and tell you how to create speed, but this TPS exercise *allows you to educate yourself* on how you naturally create the most energy. To me, that's the magic of it—allowing each player to tap into his or her power in their own way. TPS is known as one of the very top academies in the U.S. for developing power and distance in its players, and our "over-speed" work has to be a huge reason why.

Despite how demanding the work is, none of us has experienced any serious injuries from the training. John calls this "golf cardio," and it's extremely fatiguing, to the point where some kids will eventually puke from doing it. I myself never did hurl, although I came close a couple of times. I really loved that training, I guess because it made me feel like an athlete. The best part of it was that my swing was changing and I didn't even realize it!

In the Player Service we're taught that speed isn't all that valuable if you don't combine it with proper body-arm sequence. We start with creating efficient ground force reaction and reverse engineer our swings from there. One day, WGN, the national news station, came out to watch us and did a major news report on this part of our training, showing what a dramatic difference it can make.

Like a lot of juniors in TPS, I had my development accelerated thanks to John's expertise as a clubfitter. He is basically able to design and even build your equipment for you. I don't know how many coaches can do that, for sure it isn't many. I never understood why golf teachers don't know more about equipment, given it's the only thing that connects the player to ball. John's students consider it one of his secret weapons. It seems like he has an algorithm to maximize equipment for every type of player. For a variety of reasons—including the speed I can generate and the physics of how I launch the ball—I am able to hit the ball super-high, which is an asset to a certain point but can also become a liability. John customized my clubs so they are an inch shorter than standard, which gives my iron shots a piercing flight. They have a flat trajectory that optimizes my spin control and land angle.

By not having my old go-to club it would force me to develop the skill of hitting the driver.

Shortly after joining TPS, I told John that it was my dream to play Division 1 college golf. Due to my late start, it was difficult for me to imagine I could ever be a D-1 scholarship athlete. John emphasized to me that D-1 coaches typically look at driving as your potential and putting as the indicator of your mental toughness. He told me that if we mastered these two skills a coach would take a shot on me. Once I began to master John's training system, my putting improved quickly. My Achilles heel was driving accuracy. I had lots of speed which made my misses extreme. John told me this needed to change if I wanted to play Division 1.

John thinks on another wavelength. He's never afraid to trust his instincts, even if it means taking a risk with a student. He decided to configure my set of clubs so there were no fairway woods, just a driver. This was extremely risky for me as the 3-wood had been my go-to club. He told me that the best and fastest way for me to master the driver was by removing all other potential driving clubs. He said by not having my old go-to club it would force me to develop the skill of hitting the driver. He emphasized that the more I could play this way, especially in competition, the more natural the driver would become. As a result, it would become a weapon for me. Man, was he right. Along with the power I'd developed with my driver came new levels of accuracy.

In addition to this outside-the-box equipment strategy, TPS also has an amazing driving system. It's based on very in-depth research John has done to optimize three particular elements simultaneously: limiting dispersion, maximizing distance and mastering centered contact. Our facility has three bays with Trackman units, which is where this driver work takes place. All a player has to do is follow the rules of the system and Trackman will give you the feedback you need to master it. The fascinating part is having John walk you through and explain what ball flight each Trackman metric will cause. The system is super complex but very easy to apply. It is literally plug-and-play and if you put the time in, you will get the results. I have seen a lot of golfers take lessons from other teachers using technology, and no one uses it quite like TPS.

Despite my new-found success off the tee, I was never able to get my ranking high enough to get a coach to come watch me play, so John called in all his favors. He tirelessly pleaded my case to coach after coach, but no one seemed to listen. John had been one of the best golfers of all time at Florida Gulf Coast and he used his relationship there to finally get a coach to watch me. As it turned out, the coach at FGCU was blown away with my ability to drive the ball long and straight, as well as by my fast improvement curve. He took a long look and ultimately gave me my dream, a scholarship to play golf at Florida Gulf Coast University.

This was especially meaningful to me because I feel like I am following in John's footsteps—attending the same high school he went to and now being able to attend the same college. As John likes to say, "It turned out not so bad for a guy who was supposed to be the No. 6 player on his high school team."

My former classmate at St. Viator, Dana Gattone, will take it from here and explain to you the importance of the TPS principle of benchmarking.

Speed Training Video
https://www.youtube.com/watch?v=XZSLLfY55IQ

Any instructor, no matter what subject or skill they teach, knows they are in a good place if they are continually learning from their students. This comes to mind when I think of Dana Gattone and her TPS experience. Dana is one of the most charismatic people I have ever met. She is passionate, organized, warm-hearted and yet tough as nails when facing adversity. Her story is an inspiration, especially to young girls coming along behind her. Here in Dana's words is an account of our collaboration.

— J.P.

8
THE BENEFITS OF BENCHMARKING

DANA GATTONE

2014 Diane Thomason Iowa Collegiate Champion
2015 and 2016 WGCA All-American Scholar
2016 and 2017 Academic All-Big Ten
2016 and 2018 All-Big Ten Distinguished Scholar
Top 5 All-Time Illinois Player
University of Illinois Graduate

These days there is a large contingent of girls in the Player Service but, for a couple of years, I was one of only two in the program. It was just me and my best friend, Brooke Kochevar, whose twin brother Kyle is also a TPS member. When I started out, I was small for my age and not a good player. I had been a gymnast, but I was drawn to golf. In eighth grade, I made the decision to switch sports. I had hopes of making the golf team when I got to high school, but I knew I'd need to improve a lot to have any chance.

In my first few years with TPS, John tried out many of his concepts and training techniques on me, partly because I needed as much help as I could get, but also because I'm naturally very organized. He knew he could give me a lot of responsibility, and I would be diligent about following up.

I'm still a bit under five feet tall, but I became a successful Division 1 scholarship golfer at the University of Illinois. I've had the time of my life playing competitive golf and working within the TPS System to try and improve every year. My relationships with fellow TPS players are extremely important. They've had a major influence on how my life in high school and college has turned out.

At one point, I had my heart set on going to the University of Iowa, but the recruiting process was a challenge for me. I was a late bloomer, and the college coaches generally believed I was too small. It stung the most to hear that from Iowa since it had been one of my top choices. It would always motivate me when people said that, but I really had no clue how high I could set my goals. I pictured being a walk-on and slowly improving until I got to be part of the competing team as an upperclassman. Through TPS, things eventually happened quickly for me until one day, a month into my freshman year at Illinois, something pretty amazing happened. I'll explain that a little later.

Dan Kochevar, who is Kyle's and Brooke's dad, was my first golf instructor. Dan did what he could but I was really just starting out and because of my size, I had major problems finding golf clubs that fit. Dan knew John was an expert clubfitter so he recommended I go for a consultation. John set me up with irons that were frequency-matched and four degrees flat in the lie angle. He would have made them flatter if he could, as it was very difficult to get clubs short enough for me at my frequency, but any more bending and the hosels could break. He helped me fill out my set with a driver and a bunch of fairway woods that would produce 45-degree landing angles so my ball would react on the greens like the boys' shots did. Through that process of clubfitting and Dan's recommendation, John became my coach.

> My own coach, Renee Slone at University of Illinois, has been very impressed with the way the TPS System fixes my issues so quickly.

John makes complicated things simple, which helps tremendously as students get introduced to golf technology. At first, Trackman and SAM PuttLab scared the daylights out of me. There were all these numbers. I had no idea what most of them meant or any idea which one to look at first. John knew we needed to be comfortable using these high-tech tools so he developed a unique systematic way to analyze and train our swings on Trackman and our putting stroke on SAM PuttLab. He lays out a hierarchy showing which metrics to look at and how they all impact each other. My first time on Trackman I was overwhelmed, but once I learned his system, it made "neutralizing" my swing super simple. Most instructors use technology these days, but I don't think any academy uses it quite the way TPS does. On multiple occasions, I've seen top instructors and college coaches in awe of how the system can get a player to quickly manipulate the data. My own coach, Renee Slone at University of Illinois, has been very impressed with the way the TPS System fixes my issues so quickly.

Understanding the TPS Trackman system helped get me to stop hitting spinny cut shots and slices, which at the time I couldn't have done even if you had given me a million dollars. With consistent training and following the rules of the system, I developed a natural high-launch, low-spin draw and my drives eventually stretched out to 235. Thanks to a new right-to-left shot shape, accurate driving and fairway-wood play became my No. 1 skill. My accuracy with those clubs even became a running joke with the guys in TPS. In practice rounds when they would bomb their drives and we would move up to my tee, they would sometimes say, "Don't even bother hitting it, Dana, just walk out to the middle of the fairway and drop your ball there." I looked up to those guys so much, and they encouraged me all the way. When I was finally able to at least keep up with them on the course, I was pretty amazed at how far I'd come.

Once my long game was in decent shape, John was ready to take a closer look at my wedge play. In his typical honest manner, he told me it wasn't very good. His proprietary wedge system (my friend Brooke will talk more about this in the next chapter) was the structure I needed to build the necessary mechanics to improve.

> These plans, which we call "combines," include a benchmark score-based goal that can be adjusted from lesson to lesson.

We targeted the part of the golf course from about 100 yards down to 40 yards into the hole. He benchmarked my skill level as we began that part of my training, which is how we do things in TPS—practice with a testing and scoring component. This shows you very clearly where you're improving and by how much. John builds each of us a custom practice plan that we can store on our smartphones. These plans, which we call "combines," include a benchmark score-based goal that can be adjusted from lesson to lesson. Combines are tests that will give you a relative handicap based on your ability at a specific skill. John has his own way of having us track stats, which in some ways is similar to the Strokes

Gained data used on the PGA Tour. It also includes some stats no one has ever heard of. Our benchmarks for our combines are always set from our current tournament statistics.

John always studied my stats with me to identify where a specific skill improvement will improve my scoring the quickest and the most. He would point out a pattern within my rounds, such as my having a lot of par putts from six feet, and then he could show me that my strokes to hole-out rate from that distance was below average. He'd say, "Dana, we have to make you a 0-handicap golfer from six feet." If he heard me talking about how I want to get better at making mid-range putts, he would tell me that for right now it was fine for me to be a 5-handicapper from 10 to 25 feet because that part of the putting game wasn't having as big an effect on my score. It's always about zeroing in on the shortest route to lower scoring and taking the path of least resistance.

One the most important aspects of my development was becoming a great putter. Similar to the TPS Trackman system and our wedge system, John has an amazing putter training system. TPS uses Science & Motion PuttLab in conjunction with multiple training drills. Just as with Trackman, we have a hierarchy to follow when evaluating our data on the putting lab. In addition, we have a specific protocol to follow when we see a problem. Each metric on the PuttLab has a corresponding drill that will expedite a TPS student's improvement in whatever area is causing you to struggle. In my case, there were a couple of flaws that would constantly show up. To address them, John built me what we called a "stroke maintenance drill," which consisted of a few training exercises I would do every single night at home on my living room carpet. I practiced putting with a training aid that requires impact on the center of the putter face. Miss the center and you'll hit one of the clips on the toe or heel causing the ball to go sideways. I also had a training aid that goes on the floor called the Putting Arc to ensure my path stayed neutral. When he put all this together, he said to me, "This is your stroke-maintenance protocol. Do it every day and putting will be a strength of your game." Not only did I follow his instructions on the drills, I was also encouraged by John to add my own organizational tools like a whiteboard and a notebook to keep track of how many times I hit the clips or missed them. I would take the raw numbers and compute them as percentages to create benchmarks to monitor my progress. It became so valuable that, to this day, John has all his students keep customized statistics on their practice goals. It's a good feeling knowing I was able to contribute to the TPS System!

My routine all through high school was to do this drill on our living room carpet in the late afternoon while my mom was in the kitchen making dinner. It was our evening ritual and I came to look forward to it. Of course, like any kid, I would occasionally tell myself I was doing fine and didn't need to do the drill for a while. John always knew if I was fibbing when I told him I was sticking to the program. He would give me a test, and he'd know if I had done the work or not.

John knew from the beginning what a very big motivator it was for me to feel like I was on the same track as Brian, David, Tee-K and all the boys in TPS that I looked up to. After I'd reach a certain plateau in a skill area, he would introduce new segments to my program. As he was doing it, he would say something like, "This is what the guys are working on," or "I work on this exercise with David." I would be thrilled to hear that and

more eager than ever to get started on the new drill. Usually he said this in a casual, off-hand way, but not always. I remember a few times him saying to me, in a serious tone, "You've moved along far enough to be able to work on what the guys are working on, Dana." I could tell he was proud of me and was making a point of saying it. Again, it was powerful motivation.

The component of the TPS System that has made the biggest difference for me is group practice, that's a constant within TPS.

The component of the TPS System that has made the biggest difference for me is group practice, that's a constant within TPS. Everyone has rivalries with each other, and we all try to beat each other in our little competitions, but we're always rooting for one another, too. John has instilled in all of us the desire to win and compete at the best of our ability. At the same time, if we happen to lose, we want it to be to another TPS player. This to me is why we are all so close and why TPS is so much more than just a golf academy.

One day, we were doing a chipping game and I was up against one of the older boys. I chipped in twice, beating him at the game, and the other guys just loved seeing that. The boy I beat knew he was going to hear about losing to this little girl for a long time. For weeks after that, whenever I saw him, he was by the green practicing his chip shots.

John keeps reminding us that what we're doing is about golf, but it's also about much more. The longer you're in the system, the more places you go to compete and the more TPS-logo golf bags you see when you get there. When you see that logo, you automatically think, well, here's someone who speaks our language and shares our TPS attitude. You also think, here is a player who will probably be up on the leaderboard once the tournament starts. And it really does seem to work out that way.

Whenever I would go to our college tournaments, I was totally fired up about our team playing great and putting up our best possible scores so we can try to win; but once I'm on the range and I see another TPS player, I will go over and set up in the next station. Within a few minutes, the two of us will be doing our TPS thing—isolating different skills, setting up little combines and competitive games, keeping each other's numbers. . .just like a thousand times at home. When Brooke was playing for the University of Maryland and we were at the same tournament, we would always practice together on the range and putting green and do our competitions. People would scratch their heads, but eventually you could feel they were envious. It was like, wow, we want to do that, too.

The longer you're in the system, the more places you go to compete and the more TPS-logo golf bags you see when you get there.

When I went away to college as a freshman and joined the Illini women's team, I realized I was spoiled by the high level of training I'd received in the Player Service. You get a lot of structure in TPS but from the very beginning, you're taught to internalize that structure so you can organize your practice time in a disciplined way and get the most out of it. You're expected to discover things on your own, and you get the tools to do it. College is different from high school in that you get a lot of unstructured time. I would see college players trying to practice their golf efficiently, but to me it looked like they were kind of wandering around. I never doubted that I would be able to use my time well, in sports as well as in academics, which are both major priorities. I've been a Scholastic All-American and an All-Big Ten Scholar, and good time management has been a big part of that.

Obviously, when you see the end of your college years in sight, you start to feel like your time in TPS is winding down, too, but I feel I will always have close bonds with everyone who was part of it with me. My relationship with John has evolved to where he's more like an older brother to me than a coach. When I first started working with him, he hadn't even proposed to Amanda, the woman he would end up marrying. I've seen him go through that part of life where you're still single and then you get engaged, then married, and then you've got kids—all these big changes. He and I aren't all that far apart in age, and we eventually got to a point where we could communicate about any subject including all kinds of personal issues.

Of course, that wasn't possible at first because John was your typical, serious-minded 20-something guy who was pretty fixated on sports and didn't understand the emotional world of a teenage girl. One night during my senior year of high school, he had a whole bunch of us over to his house for dinner and some socializing and bonding time. As it got later and people were leaving, I kept sticking around. He seemed to realize I had something on my mind and, of course, he had noticed that I hadn't been playing well in the last few tournaments.

When we could talk privately, he asked me what was going on. I said, "John, it's my prom. I don't have a date because all the guys are scared of me because I can beat them at golf!" I broke into tears as I was blurting this out, then I looked up at him, expecting some of that great John Perna wisdom to come to my rescue.

Instead he was pretty flabbergasted. He had been expecting me to say I was worried about my golf swing or my putting stroke or about not scoring well. A moment or two went by and he still seemed somewhat shocked but at the same time, he looked relieved. In this groaning kind of voice, he said, "Oh, Dana. . .you are such a *girl*."

That was John's way of asking how in the world I could be upset about something like the prom. He did rally though. He wanted me to feel better so he reminded me what a good person I was, told me I had so much going for me, told me I shouldn't worry about something like this, and so on. It's funny to look back on, because John has changed so much. That night was important because I think deep down he knew he had a lot to learn about relating to the girls he coached, and he wanted to get better at it. I helped him in that learning process because after that night, I was never shy about telling him what was going on with me, emotionally and personally. I would talk to him about all the stuff guys just don't talk about. By the time our conversation ended that night, he had actually taken on the job of finding me a prom date, which was endearing but, in the end, turned out not to be necessary.

I mentioned that I'm an organized person, and yet my approach to the college-search process was kind of all over the map. In my junior year of high school, since I wasn't being recruited, I made a long list of schools and sent emails to about 80 coaches. I was getting emails back saying, "We've had our class picked out for two years now, sorry." I did get some encouraging responses, enough so my mom and I would get plane tickets and go visit this or that campus. But then it seemed like every time we were going down the right path, the door would close.

My prospects got a lot brighter when I qualified for the U.S. Junior Girls Championship and also the Callaway Junior World. Again, I was a little naive because I wasn't aware what a big deal these tournaments were to the college coaches.

When I got to Sycamore Hills G.C. in Ft. Wayne, Indiana for the Girls Junior, I was in a field of 150 qualifying in stroke play to continue on to match play. I ended up in the low 70s and when they posted the brackets, I was one of just two unrecruited players—the other 68 were signed to play at all these big-time schools. That left two of us for the recruiters to follow, which gave me this enormous gallery of college coaches. I was in the bottom of my bracket going against the No. 4 amateur golfer in the world, Cindy Feng, who had played in a U.S. Women's Open at age 13. I was overmatched and got off to a bumpy start, which caused a lot of the coaches to drift away. Our match ended on the 13th hole, if I remember correctly.

> My prospects got a lot brighter when I qualified
> for the U.S. Junior Girls Championship
> and also the Callaway Junior World.

But out of all this, I did get an invitation to visit Illinois and once I got there, it was suddenly the place I knew I wanted to be. Feeling certain it was the right school gave me the guts to lay out my case to the coach and tell her she had to find a spot for me. She seemed on board with everything she knew about TPS and John's approach, which was encouraging. John talked to her and showed her how I had been training and the progress I had made over the years. He said that if I didn't play as a freshman, I would still continue trending upward thanks to my TPS work, with the potential to become very competitive. I couldn't be a walk-on because at Illinois, you aren't allowed on the roster if you aren't getting some kind of scholarship package however small or large. They finally came back with an offer, and they even seemed to find money they didn't have before. I accepted and signed with them that November.

Only this seemed to present me with another problem—not being on the same level with the players I would soon be joining on the Illini women's team. On paper, the other girls were better. Because they had much higher rankings, John and I faced a new challenge. We took a calendar and flipped ahead to the following August and counted back from there, picking spots along the way where I would be aiming to reach new skill levels and performance levels. That kept me process-oriented, and the program turned out to work well. At one point early on, I had imagined having to wait until junior or senior year to play on the scoring team, but it turned out that I qualified in the top six for a first tournament. The day that happened I remember thinking, *I've gone from being a total nobody to playing on a ranked team.*

I've gone from being a total nobody to playing on a ranked team.

The third tournament on our schedule was at the University of Iowa—the school that caused me the biggest disappointment during the recruiting process. I qualified to compete and got dressed in a lot of layers for the first day's play—36 holes in windy, chilly conditions. I remembered John always telling us that miserable weather was an advantage for the mentally strong player because many people in the field would get fixated on being uncomfortable instead of hitting good shots. I figured that a couple of rounds in the mid 70s would be good enough to put me in a position to really help my team. That approach worked well and at the end of the long day, I was top-10 as an individual.

The second day was even colder, with some sleet and freezing rain. I had a secret weapon, which was a set of playing notes shared with me by my old TPS friend Brian Bullington, who was on the men's team at Iowa and knew their course well. I set up a game plan using those notes and stuck to it through the round. After I hit my tee shot on No. 16, I saw my coach come up alongside me. I was the last Illinois player on the course so she was walking me in. "Keep it up," she said, "you're right where we need you to be." It focused me even more to know I had a great chance to help our team to a high finish. I was thinking we could finish top-three or maybe even win it.

On No. 17, a par-3, my target was the entire green—sticking it close to the pin didn't enter my mind. Firing at that tucked pin would have been a complete violation of the TPS course-management system John had taught us so I wasn't going there. I hit safely on to about 25 feet, and again I stuck to a conservative mindset telling myself to lag it close, which I was able to do. I tapped in for par, went to the 18th, teed my ball and drove it down the fairway. There was a big, almost tour-style scoreboard behind that green where everybody gathers. It's very rare in college golf to have scoreboards like that so we aren't used to looking around for them. At this point, my coach wanted to be sure I didn't.

We came to my ball in the fairway, I got my yardage, pulled my 7-wood and hit the approach shot flush. It flew straight at the flag the whole way, landed softly and stopped 15 feet past the hole. I heard a loud cheer and realized how big a crowd had gathered. By the time I had my ball marked and was lining up the putt, I'd gotten word that our team had the tournament won.

I started thinking how great it would be to finish off an Illinois victory by rolling in my downhill 15-foot slider for birdie. My read was good and the stroke I made was solid but the ball ended up lipping out. As I went to tap it in, I had a twinge of disappointment about not being able to punctuate our victory by holing out. When I pulled my ball from the hole a teammate came over to me with a big smile and said, "Good job, girl! Your 76 got it done!"

I said, "I know, it's awesome. We won."

She turned back to me and shook her head and said, "No Dana, I'm saying *you* won!"

It was a team victory with me winning the individual title—a great day and one I'll always remember with a lot of pride. The most emotional part was looking at the yardage book that John made for me. He makes one for all of us when we commit to college. Each book has the TPS logo and our college logo on the cover, plus a personal motivational quote. I found myself thinking that my yardage book represented my journey in golf—my past and how far I had come. I took one last look at it then zipped it into my golf bag. In that moment, I knew that I had proved to myself and yes, to all the doubters, that I belonged.

I'm going to let my best TPS friend, and the only other girl from the original TPS crew, Brooke Kochevar, take it from here.

Brooke has been one of my toughest students to crack. Our relationship in the early days was not easy or smooth, primarily because we are so much alike. True to her nature as a highly motivated, achievement-oriented person, she stuck with the program. In the process, she helped me see that the expected path to success isn't the only path. Brooke still works closely with me at TPS, now as a coach, and I can honestly say she is one of the people I most enjoy spending time with.

—J.P.

9
THE TPS TRAINING SYSTEM FROM A DUALITY PERSPECTIVE

BROOKE KOCHEVAR

2009 and 2010 All-Midwest Team
2011 All-State
2013 Big South Presidential Honor Roll
University of Maryland Graduate

I have been playing golf for as long as I can remember having been introduced to the game by my father, Dan Kochevar, a PGA professional who believed I would benefit from the values golf instills and the rewards it provides. I've loved the game for its fun and challenges, but I've equally loved the time that my father and brother and I have been able to spend together through golf.

During those early years, however, I wasn't able to see how the game might contribute to my overall development, and I was short-sighted about opportunities it might offer me. As I was getting older and becoming a more accomplished player, I developed certain preferences about my practice and play and didn't want them disrupted. I resisted change and wanted to keep doing what felt comfortable to me.

Once my twin brother, Kyle, began having success in John's TPS training system, my parents wanted me to follow suit. It was difficult for me to wrap my mind around changing my training philosophies. With my dad as my teacher, I had experienced success in junior golf. It seemed to me that if I made a big switch, there was a decent chance it wouldn't work out well.

It's interesting that I'm looking back on those junior golf years from the perspective of my current internship with TPS, which I look to as an ideal first step toward my goal of Division 1 college coaching. One of my roles in working for John at TPS is mentoring the younger players, especially those who are about to become immersed in the college recruiting process or who already find themselves in the thick of it. I'm well qualified for this sort of counseling based on the difficult twists and turns that marked my own path into, and through, the college golf experience. And trust me, "difficult twists and turns" is a big understatement, as I'll explain.

Throughout most of high school, I was part of TPS but at the same time not part of it. I kept up my strong preference for having my father as my coach. I took part in TPS training but didn't truly commit to it. The style of training and practice John puts his players through was something I resisted at many points along the way.

Those concepts are continually evolving and undergoing refinements. One example, as explained earlier by Dan Hudson, is the way we go about "periodization," which is the separation of physical and technique development from the development of skills and mental attitudes you need in competition. Another example is the way John devises systems for all the skills a golfer needs to play high-level golf; more specifically, how he uses technology to accelerate improvement in those systems. It is also intriguing to me how so-called block and random practice function within the different TPS training systems. This was an element of golf training that took a lot of getting used to, at least for me.

I discovered in TPS that someone who has played lots of junior tournaments and worked on their game a fair amount is more devoted to "block" practice than they even realize. What is meant by "block" is that you keep repeating more or less the same shot with the same target and distance using the same club. John would tell us there is a limit to how useful this can be since in real golf you basically never face the same shot twice in a row, much less 20 times in a row. You should deal with that reality in your practice sessions by hitting a full 7-iron, then a three-quarter wedge (obviously, to a different target), then a driver that has to favor the right side, then a 5-iron under the wind, then a 3-wood that has to fade around some trees and so on.

John devises systems for all the skills a golfer needs to play high level golf.

You wouldn't figure that a junior golfer could come up with this sort of practice regimen on their own, so TPS golfers are introduced to it by having coaches stand behind them and call out the shots including which club to use. Being so used to the normal, repetitive, block style of practice, I found random practice to be strange. But observing player after player drastically improve should have made it impossible to argue with the results. What I realize now about TPS and the random form of practice is how strategically it's used. It's an excellent tool, but we don't overdo it. John would say he has us follow a hybrid system, mixing the two forms of practice according to individual need. More important to John is that we learn for ourselves when it's appropriate to apply each one.

What I eventually found so valuable about the TPS form of block practice is that it's always done as part of our core training systems. John loves systems, and he turns every aspect of our improvement into a dynamic training protocol.

Division 1 college coaches are becoming highly aware of the TPS training systems and highly impressed, as well. The coach I played for at the University of Maryland, Diane Cantu, once came to Chicago to shadow John at TPS for a day. Afterward she told me she was floored by the intricate detail of our systems,

and couldn't get over how simple they were for the players to apply.

Of all the systems in our TPS training, my favorite is the wedge system. Literally you just follow this simple protocol with a few key rules, and within an hour you can be controlling your distance within five yards. If you get a chance to try it, you'll know what I mean. It's pretty crazy how well it works. These systems always begin with block practice. Their end goal is to get you mastering some proper technique or fixing a bad habit quickly, so you can get back to skill-building and scoring.

When a TPS player has a mechanical problem or difficulties with a certain shot, they go straight to whichever system is designed to address it. In my case, the most frequent issue was ball control with my irons. Having our approach-shot system to turn to was a great feeling. It meant avoiding long segments of block practice, pounding ball after ball and guessing at what I needed to do. I would head over to our facility, jump on Trackman and apply the rules of the TPS approach-shot system. In a few minutes, I would have my problem solved. That meant I could switch back to random practice. John views swing mechanics as a "pass-fail" proposition. He drills it into his students that block practice doesn't make us better, it just allows us to be "neutral enough" with our fundamentals that we can embark on our academy's particular style of random practice, our TPS combines. Random practice with feedback and consequences is the only way a tournament player can build skills that transfer to competition. That's the idea behind it.

The coach I played for at the University of Maryland, Diane Cantu, once came to Chicago to shadow John at TPS for a day. Afterward she told me she was floored by the intricate detail of our systems, and couldn't get over how simple they were for the players to apply.

Of all John's coaching skills, his real mastery is in building these comprehensive training systems. Having a new perspective now from the coaching side, I'm even more stunned by how these systems accelerate learning. TPS spends an inordinate amount of time educating its players to ensure they understand these systems, not just the protocol, but the design and logic of each one. That education focus is a key reason there is so much buy-in from the players.

We are taught in TPS that truly acquiring a skill takes consistent effort with a mentality of "improving 1% per day."

Most golfers, including me as a junior, tend to chase that one feel or thought that will give us a big upward spike of improvement—20 or 30 or even 50% at once. John helps us understand that this approach will produce only temporary gains, which will tend to crumble under pressure. By contrast, creating a systematic plan of steady improvement, one that balances strategic block and random practice, will produce improvement that has longevity and will hold up under pressure. I learned (the hard way, usually) that this concept is 100% true!

I'm small in stature so even during my best years as a junior, I shot all my good scores on courses that required accuracy off the tee rather than length. In high school, playing from short tees on public courses, I would shoot right around par for nine holes. I once shot a 30 on a par-35 nine. In the higher-level junior tournaments on longer courses, I ended up shooting some scores that made college coaches uncomfortable.

We are taught that truly acquiring a skill takes consistent effort with a mentality of "improving 1% per day."

What distance I could achieve was greatly due to the 8-degree stiff-shafted driver John fitted me for. For a long time, I played a 13-degree driver—about as weak-lofted as they come. People will tell you that a player with low clubhead speed needs a high-lofted driver with a weak shaft in order to launch the ball high and get it to carry. In my case, those club specs caused my drives to balloon on me most of the time. I responded to that unwanted ball flight with a compensation—a downward angle of attack on the ball, which only made matters worse.

John used a combination of his driving system and

clubfitting skills to get me a driver that forced me to hit up on the ball in order to launch it to the desired height. This was particularly important to me because hitting up on the ball maximizes distance off the tee by producing the optimal mix of launch angle and spin rate. It goes without saying that any 5-foot,102-pound golfer (that's me) needs every yard they can get! John's ability to fit me into a driver that forced me to make the desired motion—versus fitting me into a club that promotes the swing flaw—was extremely risky, but a bolt of genius. Now, being on the other side of the lesson tee, I notice how he enables students to make changes without even realizing it. To me, that's the mark of a great coach.

For all my scoring challenges on longer courses, I did get an offer from a Division 1 school in the Big Ten conference, which had always been my dream. In the end, it did not work out due to circumstances that were extremely unusual and extremely traumatic for me.

What happened was I received my offer and was thrilled to accept it. I verbally committed then signed a letter of intent later that year. After that, I spent weeks talking excitedly to anyone who would listen about how great a time I would soon be having at college. A couple of months after I'd signed my letter, the coach called me with horrible news. The offer had been rescinded. The reasons they gave didn't make sense to me then and years later, they still don't add up. But there was nothing to be done about it.

Neither before that day nor since have I ever received a phone call so shocking and awful. I can tell you exactly where I was standing when the phone rang. I can tell you exactly what I was wearing and what the weather was like, every detail of the moment. I went from feeling on top of the world to feeling like a worthless outcast.

I mentioned earlier about being jolted out of my comfort zone, well, that's the event that jolted me. I was shocked and embarrassed, but I was also angry and motivated to show people what a mistake this had been. I turned to John and told him that if he would help me, I was ready to pick myself off the ground and start working toward my true potential as a golfer. He always tells us, "Life isn't fair," then he usually adds that "everything happens for a reason." I asked for a new practice plan and vowed to follow it faithfully.

Of course, I was also in a position of having to find a new school—not so easy when it's already February of your senior year. I did some scrambling and ended up getting an opportunity at Coastal Carolina University, which is a wonderful place. I loved the CCU campus, loved my coach and teammates, loved being near the beach and, on top of all that, I was thrilled to have an opportunity to prove myself.

Despite my love for Coastal, I still harbored a goal of playing Big Ten golf. It was all part of wanting to prove I had been wrongly treated and deserved to play at that level. This desire kept me training hard during my freshman season at CCU and in the off-season as well. Coincidentally, this was just about the time John developed TPS Collegiate, an extension of his junior program. TPS Collegiate is a pretty seamless continuation of the TPS junior program, but it requires increased attention to detail and it calls for additional self-discipline on the part of the player. I immersed myself in my extended TPS training and thought often of John's trademark phrase: "A golfer has to *love the process* of getting better."

I committed myself to a daily training regimen of structured skill acquisition through the TPS System, and eventually earned the opportunity to become a scholarship athlete at the University of Maryland. This was a dream come true for me.

My path was neither easy nor conventional, but I wouldn't change it for the world. I recognize that adversity and the many twists in my path have been instrumental in making me the person I am today. I believe it's important to look back at life experiences and allow those experiences to guide you. In doing that, I'm able to see the various reasons why I've gravitated toward coaching.

My experiences in high school and college, both positive and negative, have enabled me to relate with compassion and with a lot of motivational energy to young people who are working their way through the recruiting process. Thanks to my experience as a TPS player and now via my internship in the academy, I feel I've been getting a doctorate in the process of developing golfers into players!

The only person who has been in TPS longer than my brother and I is Joey Carlson. Joe will take the story from here. You'll be reading the words of someone else who is taking his experience in TPS and as a Division 1 player and applying it to a profession other than golf.

As you'll find out in reading his contribution to this book, Joe Carlson came to TPS before it was fully established. More than just a phenomenal golfer, Joe is also extremely intelligent and an all-around high achiever. I'll always cherish my time working with Joe, and I know for certain he is destined to do great things in this world.

—J.P.

10
WHAT'S
YOUR
FREQUENCY?

2008 Individual State Champion/Scoring-Record Holder
2008 Illinois Junior Player of the Year
2014 Srixon/Cleveland All-America Scholar
2014 West Coast Conference All-Academic
University of San Diego Graduate

The story of my involvement with the Player Service is different from other stories told in this book. I became part of TPS before it was TPS. I like to call that the "beta time." It was a period when John was constantly researching and testing cutting-edge concepts, things I'd never seen or heard of in the game of golf.

John and I have a lot in common. We both attended St. Viator High School and we played for the same golf coach there, Jack Halpin. Like John, I had Dan Kochevar as my swing coach during the early stages of my junior career. John and I figured out quickly that we're both *uber*-competitive and have a tendency to get hot-headed out on the course. I think that's why our initial connection was so strong. I can honestly say that without the guidance and support of John and Dan there is no way I would have won a state championship, nor would I have gotten the opportunity to play Division 1 golf.

That's a little-known fact: TPS golfers play a single ball position, 3-iron through wedge.

I'm a recreational golfer now, having finished out my very rewarding NCAA career at the University of San Diego and moved on to DePaul University College of Law where I'm completing my final year. As much as John steered me and supported me through the challenges of D-1 golf competition, he also imparted a lot of guidance that applies to this part of my life and career. I've found his teaching and mentoring to be relevant to all the different ways that life tests us and challenges us.

Studying the law focuses your mind on what is factual and how it can be proven. My experience inside the Player Service had a similar effect on me. But since TPS was so new and unknown at the time I trained there, it also taught me that what's factual and provable can be found in unlikely places. In any dialogue or debate, ideas and institutions that are well-known and long-established get an automatic leg up. Longevity probably should earn you the benefit of the doubt, but nothing more. In no way does it give you a monopoly on what is provably true.

For evidence, you can look at what TPS does in the realm of golf equipment for its players. I'm a scratch golfer and while I don't compete anymore, I still love to play. Plus, I went to college down the road from what is the hub of the U.S. golf equipment industry, Carlsbad, California. Yet I still have never been able to find new golf clubs to replace the ones that were custom-fitted and custom-built for me seven years ago.

Nothing I try can match the performance of my TPS set—not in clubhead speed, ball speed, distance or dispersion. They aren't new and shiny anymore, but they still give me the most profound advantage a golfer can ask for—never having to hit balls in order to "find the feel" of the various clubs in my set. My clubs provide a second big advantage: never having to move the ball up and back in my stance based on which club I'm hitting.

> I've found his teaching and mentoring to be relevant to all the different ways that life tests us and challenges us.

Yes, that's a little-known fact: TPS golfers play a single ball position, 3-iron through wedge. This is in good part because the clubs in each player's bag all have the same frequency as measured in cycles per minute (CPMs) on a device known as a frequency analyzer. They are "frequency-matched" but in finished form with the clubheads and grips attached. If you take an interest in golf gear, you've certainly heard about frequency-matching as a quality-control feature that basically means all shafts—whether they're rated "stiff" or "regular" or "senior," etc.—will have extremely tight tolerances as to their flexibility. Important point: This refers to the shafts in their raw, uncut form, as they arrive from the factory. Once you take them out of the box and start cutting them to length and installing heads on them—heads that have differing gram weights, 3-iron through the wedges—you're on your way to a set of clubs with unmatched frequencies.

When John first worked with me, he looked at my golf bag and asked me if I had a "matched set" of clubs. I said yes and showed him the "S-400" label on all the shafts. We went into his shop and put my clubs on the frequency analyzer. The CPM readouts were all different. The numbers went up as the clubs got shorter, meaning a club such as my 3-iron was considerably more flexible than my 9-iron.

He asked, "Are you trying to make the same golf swing with each club?" I told him I was, and he told me that made good sense. A golfer wants the same "release pattern" from club to club is the reason why. Frequency dictates how the club loads and unloads in the backswing and forward swing, producing kick at the bottom of the swing, where impact occurs. If all frequencies in a set of clubs are the same, the desired release pattern can remain constant on every shot.

"You want optimum deflection at the bottom with every club," he told me, 'based on a release pattern that is optimal for your own particular way of moving your body and moving the club." The traditional way of building a set of clubs, where the shorter clubs are stiffer than the longer clubs, makes no sense in John's view, other than the fact that it is "10 times more difficult and time-consuming," in his words, to assemble a set that's frequency-matched in finished form.

Now, I should mention, even though every student goes through the fitting process, we are under no compulsion to switch out the clubs we came with and start playing our TPS-fit and TPS-built clubs. As John was fitting me, he made the point that the equipment facet of his work with me was exactly like every other aspect of the work we'd do together—it's completely based on results. "If these clubs don't beat the clubs you have now," he told me, "they will not go in your bag."

The clubs I was playing when I came to TPS were

top-of-the-line and they were fitted to me by the top clubfitting company in Chicago. But as I came to discover, they were contributing to some inconsistencies in how I made contact and how the ball flew. With my new clubs, I could play off a single ball position. "On my heart," is how we describe it, meaning just left of my sternum. After that, everything felt so much smoother and easier. I felt my approach to the game of golf suddenly get much simpler. Very soon after I got these clubs, I went down to Bloomington, Illinois to play in our state high school championship. I not only won the title, I also set a scoring record for the tournament, which stands to this day.

> If all frequencies in a set of clubs are the same, the desired release pattern can remain constant on every shot.

When you're custom-fit by TPS, all the test clubs are built with proprietary shafts—a steel one for irons and a graphite one for woods. They are all identical in their raw state, based on all having the same "EI profile." In golf shafts, EI profile is basically a "fingerprint." The E stands for "modulus of elasticity," meaning the stiffness of the material, and the I stands for "area moment of inertia," a measure of stiffness of the cross-section of the shaft. The TPS fitting system has researched hundreds of shafts and come up with its own EI profile to base everything off.

Clubfitting at TPS is based on the 4-iron and the 9-iron. Lie angle is factored in as you test various 4-irons and 9-irons, but the frequency of the finished club—when you are handed the club that is right for you—is the real eureka moment. When that happened for me, the feeling at impact was amazingly pure. The ball flight was perfect. My club speed was up, ball speed was up, and as I hit a long series of shots the dispersion pattern that resulted was extremely tight. This was with a 9-iron. Next, I hit a group of test 4-irons. When I got to the 4-iron that is right for me, the same great results all happened. John took the 9-iron and the 4-iron and placed them on the frequency analyzer, and the CPMs matched exactly. In my old set, my 9-iron and 8-iron differed by five CPMs; the 9-iron and 4-iron were more than 30 CPMs apart.

> Put me through a blind test of my club and
> an identical club that differs by two CPMs,
> and I will never fail that test.

When a player has completed the fitting process at TPS, John will sometimes hand them a 7-iron that's exactly like the 7-iron they'll be carrying in their bag, except it's stiffer or more flexible by two CPMs. Two CPMs is, obviously, a tiny increment. But a player can feel it. Now when you're using a traditional set, the brain will recognize the differences in length and those length variations will trigger manipulations. It happens at a subconscious level, you aren't aware of these subtle compensations you're making. Changing ball position and changing your release pattern are common forms of this manipulation.

As John explained to me, the pattern in a well-made traditional set is that the CPMs differ in even increments, so I suppose the compensation and manipulations you have to make would be less random. But once you hit a set in which every club is the same frequency, even the slightest variation in CPMs is noticeable. Put me through a blind test of my club and an identical club that differs by two CPMs, and I will never fail that test. That's how precisely the human body and brain and nervous system are wired. It blew my mind when I realized that such a tiny difference could be felt. "Even hackers can tell the difference," John will sometimes say, and it's true.

When I played my traditional set with its varying frequencies, I noticed that I needed to hit lots of balls in warmup, especially if I had put the clubs aside for a little while. That's about re-programming a whole bunch of minor compensations to try and get decent performance out of your non-frequency-matched set of golf clubs. It's such a relief not to have to go through that anymore. Once I went through the fitting and had my TPS set of clubs, the game became much easier for me. Golfers don't realize all the small contortions they must constantly re-groove, based on differences from one club to another. The equipment you play as a TPS golfer addresses that problem.

It's the same idea behind the TPS approach to swing mechanics. "Now you can learn how to play golf," John will always say, once an equipment problem or a problem with swing mechanics gets solved. He doesn't want us to hit 30 8-irons to find the little manipulations we need to make simply because our clubs aren't what they should be. That's a complete waste of time, and TPS is a system in which time is valued like gold. Tournament golf is a complex activity, and there's a lot you have to learn to compete at your potential: how to plan a shot, how to execute it, how to move around the golf course, how to scramble, how to respond to all the situations you find yourself in. We spend our time on those things.

John worked intently with me on the mental game, and he was able to get some very helpful concepts ingrained in me. I recognized my weaknesses in putting and the short game, and we worked on those together. The importance of keeping your strengths intact while improving areas where you're weak was a priority with him. "Your strengths have to be maintained, Joe," he'd often tell me. That makes sense no matter what you're doing in life, in part because your strengths are what give you self-confidence.

I was open to being challenged by John and held accountable, which is how he operates anyway. As others have said, you can see the wheels turning in his head all the time as he looks for ways to help you play better and compete more successfully. But at the same time, he is also trying to teach maturity. He's looking for the right way to do that with each different student. I'm sure he decided early on that if a student isn't becoming a more mature and responsible person, he or she won't achieve their potential in golf tournaments or in life.

At the core of TPS, there are two messages: First, time is the most valuable commodity in the world, so that anything—from equipment to technology—that can accelerate the learning process and thus open up more time to develop skills, should be taken advantage of. Second, our success depends on being forced to set goals and work toward them diligently, in the process gaining a true appreciation of ourselves, our capacities and the value of the people around us.

Obviously, golf is a game of results. At the same time, it's a process, a pretty long and gradual process. Along the way, a coach can instill important qualities in a student that will serve that student well on the golf course or in any other area of life. I don't talk much about playing collegiate golf with the people I've met in law school, but the ones who know me best know that it left a big imprint on me. That goes even more so for TPS and the training I received there. It made college golf possible, not to mention extremely enjoyable, and it's been invaluable to me as I've moved forward to take on the many challenges of law school.

During my time at TPS, I always wished the training facility was closer to where I lived, which would have saved me the 45-minute trip through traffic to get my training in. But I could never complain about it to Joo-Young Lee, a fellow TPS golfer whose commute was seven hours each way. Acquiring the ability to learn independently is a priority at TPS, and Joo-Young truly exemplifies that. He tells the unusual story of his training and development in this next chapter.

No two people have the same personality or the same learning style. Joo-Young Lee was the first true introvert I worked with. The challenge of getting player and father to buy in was difficult but it was an opportunity I relished. Joo sacrificed a lot to train with TPS, including having to travel hundreds of miles each way.

— J.P.

11
SELF
DISCOVERY

2012 AJGA All-American
2012 US Junior Semi-Finalist
2014 Big East All-Academic Team
2015 Ohio State Amateur Champion
2015 MAC All-Academic Team
2016 and 2018 All MAC Tournament Team
Northern Illinois Graduate

If your goal is to play golf at the highest levels, you can easily fall into the trap of over-analyzing your swing. At some point, every serious player probably does that—gets too technical. I know I did. A lot of people will advise you to keep it simple. They'll tell you not to let your swing thoughts get too complicated.

That sounds very wise. But the person who offers that wisdom has to be able to back it up. A coach needs to be able to point out one adjustment their student needs to make, then give the player a

JOO-YOUNG LEE

way to actually make that adjustment, with the result that one change clears up five or six problems or flaws. To me, that's the sign of true excellence in coaching, and it's what John Perna's training system has been able to do for me.

The idea for me to become part of the Player Service came about during an AJGA tournament in which TPS player Tee-K Kelly played very well and had a high finish. I wasn't playing very well at the time and my father got curious about Tee-K's development. I had competed in junior tournaments with him over the years and had generally outplayed him. Now Tee-K had seemed to pass me, and my dad wanted to know who his coach was. In talking to John about him possibly becoming my coach, I was very encouraged. I had a sense he could change how I approached tournament golf and training in general in a way that might bring out my true potential. John ended up doing just that, although it was extremely difficult for me to wrap my head around his concepts and get myself to fully believe in them.

I realize now that John didn't so much teach me something as allow me to discover something.

I grew up as the only child of caring and very serious-minded parents. In particular, I had the influence of a perfectionist father. I ended up as a junior golfer who went around thinking golf really *is* a game of perfect, or at least it could be.

I could never motivate myself to practice recovery shots because I so hated missing greens and fairways. The whole idea of learning to scramble for pars felt like admitting defeat. TPS has a lot of excellent concepts that go into John's coaching system and how we train; when I came to him I didn't understand any of them. My approach to the game was to hit the ball perfectly straight and on-target every time in order to make birdie on every hole. John had the hard job of getting me to unlearn that. It was very deeply ingrained in me. Eventually, my own perfectionist ways required a conversation between the two of us that lasted all through the night. I was staying at John's house when this particular conversation began one evening, and it didn't end until the sun was coming up. That's what it took for me to finally let go of my old paradigm about how to train and compete.

One reason it was so hard for him to rewire my brain about practice and competition is that I had played from an early age and been successful. In my first few years of junior golf, I shot low scores and I won more than my share of tournaments. I was an early bloomer. But by the time I was ready for high school, I had really tailed off.

When I made the commitment to accept John's belief system and find my way back to success via TPS, it created a couple of hardships. The first involved geography. We lived just outside Columbus, Ohio, and that's about 350 miles east of Chicago. My parents and I would get up early on Saturday mornings and make the drive. It's a little less than seven hours, and we did it every week. For my dad to get on the same page with John's ideas was very difficult. John knew he had to challenge the father-son connection in my family. He did it in subtle, steady ways that weren't confrontational. Before long, my dad didn't have a problem with how John was teaching me because the results were very good, and my dad really liked those results. My father and my coach aren't at all similar in how they think, but my dad came around. He actually finds John fun to talk to now.

As I said, my game was in bad shape when I started in TPS, and then quickly got better. Within a year, I had made the semi-finals of the U.S. Junior Boys, I won on the AJGA Tour, and ended up an AJGA All-American.

> Within a year, I had made the semi-finals of the U.S. Junior Boys, I won on the AJGA Tour, and ended up an AJGA All-American.

John's style in training me was influenced by a few factors, including how far away I lived. "Self-discovery" is a major belief with TPS, and I was probably the poster boy for that. When we worked one-on-one, our sessions were short. Instead of standing at the tee with me for an hour, he kept our sessions to about 15 minutes. He would give me an outline of what to work on and tell me the criteria for whether I was getting the message—either certain numbers I needed to hit on Trackman or certain ball flights I would need to see while doing a drill. In putting, it would be the feedback from the SAM PuttLab numbers and the results of my combines.

He taught me the value of doing a lot of reps, trusting the process as I went along. He told me later that he would have stayed with me on the tee for an hour or more, but he saw that I didn't really engage with the drill he had assigned as long as he was standing there. My tendency when he was there was to let him "connect the dots" on what I was doing and what the results were. He knew I needed to connect those dots myself. I realize now that John didn't so much teach me something as allow me to discover something.

That was how TPS worked in my particular case. John knew

I was comfortable working on my own and he saw me as a student who, even more than most others, needed to figure this out in my own way. "The only thing that will hold up under pressure is what you find out for yourself," he would tell me. "Any swing feelings or swing thoughts I try to give you will be a lot less powerful than the ones that come to you during self-discovery."

I received a full scholarship to play college golf at Xavier University down in Cincinnati. That put me in a new environment with a whole different kind of daily schedule, which meant no more long drives to Chicago to work with John. I felt I still needed a swing coach and began working with one whose approach was more traditional, and by that I mean more technical. There were more swing positions to try to get to and there was more analysis of how my swing was hitting those positions or not hitting them. Obviously, there was far less self-discovery. The results weren't positive, and my play went downhill. My scores were drifting up into the 80s.

It was obvious that my initial experience with TPS had allowed me to completely revive my game. It was clear that I needed to recommit to the style of training I had received there. John and I talked about me transferring from Xavier up to Northern Illinois University, which was a program on the rise and a setting that would finally put me in close proximity to TPS. There were conversations with the NIU coach, who was having to look at my play as a Xavier freshman and somehow had to see a player who could help his team. John told him those scores weren't indicative of my talent, and I ended up at Northern Illinois and back in the TPS program. The results once again were positive. I got off to a difficult start in my first season as a transfer but improved to finish with my best scores of the year.

At NIU, I managed to become the first Huskie in program history to earn All-Midwest Region honors from the Coaches Association. I set new scoring records for a single round—a 65—and for a 54-hole tournament—a 202 total. I've been a first-team All-MAC honoree and twice been named MAC Golfer of the Week. I had low scoring average on my team as a junior at 73.72. Most important to me was winning my first collegiate tournament at the Desert Shootout Collegiate, where I set those two scoring records.

The summer before my junior year of college, I achieved the greatest single-event success of my golf career so far—winning the Ohio Amateur Championship in a playoff. It was held at Zanesville Country Club in mid-July. I came into it feeling some positive momentum about my play. I shot an even-par 72 the first round, which left me about six strokes off the lead. The next day I shot a 69, including a chip-in for birdie, and I was just a few strokes back at the halfway point of the tournament.

In the third round, I gave those three strokes back. Conditions were difficult that day with gusty winds, so scores were up in general. My round consisted of 16 pars and a two-hole stretch on the back nine where I went bogey-double. It was a 75, but it seemed survivable, as I was still just four shots off the lead. I knew most of the guys I'd be up against, so there was no mystery just a matter who could play their best golf.

That week, I was staying at a teammate's house in Marietta, Ohio about 70 miles south of the course. He wasn't in contention at that point so his tee time was early and he got up early to drive solo to Zanesville. I set my alarm for a later wake-up and got a good night's sleep. At least I think I set my alarm because the first thing I remember from that morning was my friend's mom peeking her head into the room and saying, "Aren't you supposed to be at the golf course, Joo-Young?"

I had overslept. And now I had a problem. There was still time to get to the course if nothing went wrong like getting a speeding ticket. I had no choice but to drive down Interstate 77 at 80 miles an hour the whole way, but I didn't get stopped and I didn't hit traffic so I started to get my head back on straight as I got near the end of the ride. In the end, I was able to hit a few balls, hit some putts and get to the tee in plenty of time. During my warm-up, I could hear John's voice in my head shouting at me, "Don't panic, Joo-Young, just trust your training."

One of the fundamentals of TPS training is to choose generous targets and "swing fearlessly." At the point in my career when the 2015 Ohio Amateur came along, I had finally internalized that concept. Having so little pre-round preparation time made that belief about no-fear all the more important and all the more logical to me. I teed my ball up and hit it as hard as I could down the middle of the fairway. The hole was a reachable par-5, and I hit my second shot just as hard onto the green. I had a very long first putt and didn't lag it all that well so I started off with a three-putt for my tap-in par. My only thought was "Fine. Let's go to No. 2."

At NIU, I managed to become the first Huskie in program history to earn All-Midwest Region honors from the Coaches Association.

I was in a good place, and my intense love of tournament competition was causing a real good energy to flow through me. Things went well from there and I ended up shooting 68, which was low round of the day. It got me to 4-under for the tournament and into a two-man playoff, which I won with a birdie on the first playoff hole. I was interviewed by reporters afterward and, at first, I was at a loss for words. The Ohio

Amateur is a tournament I had only dreamed of winning, It was a truly special day for me and for my parents, as well, who have done so much to support my golf career. I was thinking that it was also a good day for TPS because it once again helped prove how many different types of golfers John's system is able to train for success.

As I said earlier, I joined TPS because of the success Tee-K Kelly was having. Tee-K and I are also linked together by the fact that in 2015 I won the Ohio State Amateur and he won the Illinois State Amateur, which was a very cool double-down for TPS. If you've ever had to learn a hard lesson about motivation and commitment, what Tee-K shares in the upcoming chapter will hold a lot of meaning for you.

Tee-K is like my non-biological son. He is intense and aggressive and has a short fuse. He is also one hell of a competitor. Tee-K has challenged me mentally, emotionally and strategically as a coach. It's been exhilarating to see him climb to the top. He has filled a particular void in me; I feel I was put here to help him navigate around the pitfalls I experienced as a player.

—J.P.

12
"S**T OR
GET OFF THE POT"

2013 and 2015 Illinois State Amateur Champion
2016 NCAA Division 1 All-American
2016 NCAA Regional Champion
2017 Dominican Republic Open Champion
(PGA Tour Latinoamérica)
2017 Bupa Challenge Champion
(PGA Tour Latinoamérica)
2018 Web.com Tour Member
Ohio State University Graduate

Athletes have different personality types. Some are extremely competitive with a fiery intensity they can't hide. That was always me. Some are hard workers, so-called gym rats and range rats. I believe it's possible for a young athlete to display both those traits—steadiness and dedication plus the burning passion to win.

But looking back to my high school days, I can see that I did not possess a true work ethic. In hindsight, I would say I misread my competitive fire for genuine commitment to the process of getting better. I was such an intense competitor that I *thought* I was a hard worker. I will never forget the night I learned this wasn't the case.

My coach, John Perna, showed up at my house in the middle of family dinner, unannounced. The impromptu meeting that soon took place would change the path of my golf career dramatically.

This was the summer before senior year of high school. We were sitting at the table about to eat when I heard a bang on the door. It was John. None of us expected him so my parents and I were curious about the purpose of his visit. It was a night never to forget. John had some things to say about my approach to golf training, and he didn't beat around the bush. You might even say he laid into me. He literally told me it was time to *"S**t or get off the pot."*

He had come to our house to deliver a strong message, and I can appreciate now the risk he took in speaking so plainly. He came to tell me what I needed to hear. And no, I did not like hearing it, not one bit. He said I was too talented a golfer to be playing at the level I was playing. "You think you're better than you are," John told me. "You get outworked by players with less ability. You're getting lapped by these guys, and you don't even realize it."

He went on, "You're an athletic kid who can generate clubhead speed and you have a wonderful feel for the game but your swing is very inefficient," he said. "Your impact conditions are very poor, you add too much loft to every shot. You think you're going places as a golfer, but I gotta tell you, Tee-K, the way things are now, you're going nowhere."

I sat there and didn't speak much, but I was getting steamed up. I had only been working with him for a couple of months and I knew he was a good coach, but at the dinner table that night I wasn't thinking anything good about John Perna. I sincerely believed that the way I was going about my business was OK. I had been the Illinois Golf Association Junior Player of the Year in 2008. I made the MAJGT All-Midwest team in 2010. In so many games, in all different sports, I had won as a kid many times because I wanted it more than the other guy. I know that my hatred of losing is stronger than just about anybody's. Once the bell would ring, I seldom, if ever, got outworked.

But obviously, in the long run, that isn't enough. The real work takes place before and after competitions.

After John left, I turned to my parents hoping for some support. I had my arms folded across my chest, and I was shaking my head. I had a look on my face that basically said, "What the hell was all that about?"

I could see they were taken aback, same as I was, but they weren't saying the same things I was saying. They felt John had spoken the truth. They weren't going to take my side and reject his comments about me. They were actually on board with what he said.

I should point out that my mother was a top-rank collegiate golfer in her day. She played on the University of Tulsa team that won the women's NCAA championship in 1988. That experience gives her a different perspective than what a lot of parents might bring. The truth was, coaches from the bigger Division 1 programs were out recruiting high school juniors and they weren't recruiting me. It had been my dream to play high-level D-1 college golf, and I wasn't getting recruited by those programs.

In a golf tournament, you get into positions where you have to take some risk. You rely on instinct to decide when that moment is, then you trust your feeling and take your shot. That's what John had done as a coach that night—he took a risk, he took his shot. His message got heard.

My parents pointed out all the positives in what he had

said. Being told you have way above-average talent isn't so bad, right? Being told you have competitive fire is yet another good thing. Having the coach say you have a rare ability to hole out from all over the course, and that you could "will the ball into the hole" is good, as well. Being told that you will always play your best golf when you're in contention is also positive. I appreciated all that.

It's just that no athlete—I don't care who you are—wants to be told by a coach they've been dogging it.

One reason I felt I was doing what I needed to do was that I had quit other competitive sports in order to commit to golf exclusively. In hindsight, I now realize that I had faded from those other sports because I couldn't excel at them, and that didn't work with my competitiveness. Or my self-image, I suppose.

After that night, things changed. My eyes were opened, and I was suddenly a much better listener. John noticed the change. He saw I was now willing to do whatever it would take to reach my potential. He created a program that the "old me" would not have been willing to accept, with very basic drills that had to be repeated constantly. At the very beginning, I did indeed have thoughts go through my head about how I might get out of doing them. But that was over very quickly. In fact, this came to be the point in time when I understood how much I cared about golf. The love I always had for the game, everything about it, got channeled into this training program.

It all revolved around a series of drills, addressing all aspects of my game. All through that summer before senior year, with new-found motivation from John's speech, I would grind out these drills every single day. One drill in particular stood out. It was pretty simple—golf swings with an alignment stick planted in the ground a foot or so off my right hip. On the takeaway, my clubhead had to go outside that stick and on the downswing, it had to travel inside the stick. For months and months, I wasn't allowed to take a swing on the range without that orange stick next to me.

Like so many full-swing drills in golf, it exaggerates the move and the feeling it's designed to create. This drill was a pretty extreme over-exaggeration, but it had to be done thousands of times over. People would come up to me on the range at Medinah Country Club (our family's club) and say things like, "That's a pretty crazy-looking drill" and "You're not actually going to try to swing like that, are you?" True, it was goofy-looking, and it felt to me like an enormous loop, but like a lot of drills John gives his players, it allowed me to hit very good shots almost right away.

I say "almost" because at first all I could do was hit three-quarter wedge shots with a lazy kind of swing. Anything more and I had no chance to swing on the required path. Still, even with three-quarter pitching wedges, I would hit that stick with my hands quite often. The challenge in the early days was to avoid having sore knuckles and dark bruises all over the backs of my hands. As time went on, the swing path I was supposed to be following got grooved by that orange stick and that simple drill. I got so I could hit full drivers and not really think about contacting the stick.

There was a moment along the way when I realized, "This is just reps. This is all about doing something a certain number of times." That got me even more motivated because I knew I was willing to put in the work. Another motivator was what the drill did to my clubface angle through impact. I was always a "hands player" with very good feel for what my hands and the clubhead were doing at any given time. With this drill, as I built muscle memory relative to swing direction, it got so the clubface could only do one thing—come square at impact. I was hitting from the same position every time and striking the ball flush. The face would be dead square at impact and the ball flight would be dead straight.

> With this drill, as I built muscle memory relative to path, it got so the clubface could only do one thing—come square at impact.

Still, that was on the practice tee. I had tournaments to compete in and a lot to prove in a short period of time. My back was up against the wall that summer. So I got the notion into my head of at least attempting, in tournament play, to execute the "end goal" swing John had planned for me. Obviously, this full-scale swing overhaul wasn't going to be completed in a few months. (More like a few years is how it actually turned out.) But in the meantime, what was I going to do in competition?

John told me three things. He said that trying to execute the end-goal swing wouldn't work in competition because I would be out there with lots of mechanical thoughts bouncing around my head, which would result in great difficulty in achieving my ultimate performance state. He also told me that *being in the midst of a swing overhaul was not an excuse to finish poorly in events.* It was still my responsibility to go out and perform. He also reminded me that I was the rare type of golfer who didn't have to be striking the ball well to shoot low scores.

I was frustrated because the drills had given me a taste of what it was like to flush my shots and fire them on a powerful, controlled trajectory, instead of ballooning everything. I kind of whined that I had worked hard, and I was starting to hit the ball well on the range. . .and now what, I can't try and bring this new move into competition? He reminded me about my unusual ability to scramble, my way of never giving up on a hole, my ability to hole out basically no matter what. "You take that strength and you make it stronger, Tee-K," he told me. "If you do that, what's going to happen when the swing change is completed? I'll tell you what's going to happen—*no one is going to be able to beat you.*"

I came away from those conversations feeling a sense of urgency and a deep desire to compete, no matter what the state of my golf swing was. The next tournament I played in, an Illinois junior event, I went out and won. A week later, I went to an AJGA tournament in Wisconsin and nearly won that, too. But on the home stretch, my foot slipped on a drive, right at the top of my backswing, resulting in an 80-yard tee shot. A freak occurrence; otherwise, that event was probably mine, as well.

A few weeks later, I entered the Illinois Open and finished in the top 10. I remember I made eight birdies in the final round, being paired with and actually scoring lower than the University of Illinois coach, Mike Small, who is known as a very good tournament player. My whole trajectory had changed. In two months, I went from being the No. 3,000-something junior player in the country to somewhere in the top 40.

My big moment came in an AJGA event in Ohio, the 2011 Columbus Junior, which is played on the Scarlet Course at Ohio State University. By the time I got there, John and I had agreed on a full-swing strategy in which I was basically hitting a knock-down style shot—off the tee, and from the fairway. I would be taking my hands back to shoulder height and they would finish at shoulder height. I had the ball just a little bit back in my stance, though not all the way to the right heel, and I was trapping everything. This was a shorter action and a simplified move back and through, one I could easily repeat. I should mention that my swing motion John was so critical of had always caused me to hit the ball absurdly high. Now with this variation of the classic knock-down, my shots were flighting like most players. I wasn't ballooning the ball, I was hitting it with a nice flat trajectory.

I ended up winning the Columbus AJGA tournament. This was especially important to me because Ohio State was my top choice among schools to attend. I was using a makeshift golf swing, but my competitive fire was the same as ever. It burns hotter when I'm playing well, which I feel sets me apart from a lot of other golfers. John calls this my "ability to finish." I'm never scared of winning. If anything, my issue is getting too pumped up so that I might make a questionable decision. But I've never been in contention and been "feeling it" and then become doubtful. I don't watch a fellow-competitor and think, I hope this guy misses because I don't think I'll make it. I can spot the player who is doing that and be pretty sure they are headed down the leaderboard, not up, which is how it usually turns out.

Another game-changer for me is John's ability to train me mentally and the approach he takes to that. I'm not a player who should try to maintain an "even keel" emotionally. John has told me that I'm his "non-biological son." I'm the student in TPS who is most like him in terms of getting heated up in competition. Neither of us is any good at trying to stay cool. I turned out to be the player who most proved his theory that you can't try to change a golfer's personality. "I'm not going to give you breathing exercises, Tee-K," he would tell me. "You are going to show your emotions out there—it's your nature. You aren't Ernie Els or Jason Dufner, and you never will be—you've got to be yourself."

What's interesting is that I never, ever feel more like myself—more like the real Tee-K—than when I am playing well in a tournament and turning up the heat, amping up the passion, going for a victory.

The highlight of junior golf for me was earning a scholarship to Ohio State. I was extremely grateful and proud of achieving that goal, especially given how far along I was in my high school career before I began to excel. I remember when I was making my commitment to OSU, I told John, "My goal now is to become a Division 1 All-American." He told me in a calm way this was a wonderful goal, but my ball-control skills were not strong enough—not yet anyway—for me to achieve it. There he was with more candid feedback, and again it motivated me.

My work with John on my golf swing continued into junior year of college, believe it or not. I learned to "let the drills affect my swing organically," as John puts it. In other words, I would simply keep doing the drills John would lay out for me and never think about mechanics when I compete. He told me that over time, the only way for a change to hold up under pressure is for it become part of my "DNA," and for that to happen, it takes commitment and consistency in training. He would say, "You don't rush it, you don't get impatient, you trust that you'll absorb it." Which in the end is what happened for me. Now we don't work on my swing anymore.

Meanwhile, what John told me back in high school about making my strength stronger continued to hold true. During my career at Ohio State, we would, like the players on any other college team, qualify to be part of the competing squad for the next tournament. In many of those qualifiers, I would be hitting it all over the place and shooting a lower score than teammates whose ball-striking happened to be very good that day. I saw how much it irritated them, and I would use that to my advantage. I had days where I missed 11 greens and recovered to inside five feet every single time. I would short-side myself in a bunker and splash it to six feet and make that six-footer. The next hole I would make a 20-footer to save par, and I would know the putt was in the whole way.

> You don't rush it, you don't get impatient,
> you trust that you'll absorb it.

There were times I would get the spot and a teammate would come up to me and say, "I played so much better than you and here you end up beating me for the spot." I would tell him that didn't make sense. How could he play better golf than I was playing and still shoot a higher score? Playing good golf means shooting a good score. Playing great golf means shooting a great score. I would tell my teammate he had hit the ball better than I had, but he hadn't played better. If he had, his score would have been lower than mine. End of story. If you want a higher authority on this point, think about a Jack Nicklaus quote that John has been fond of repeating: "The greatest and toughest art in golf is 'playing badly well.'"

John and I had a unique situation in that he had to do so much intense coaching of me, even after I left Chicago and went off to Ohio State. We developed a routine where I would call him on the eve of any final round of an event at about 10 p.m. For me, the day's round wouldn't be officially over until we had our conversation about it. He has a way of looking at what's going on, hearing about my play and saying things like, "You're hitting it well, you're putting well, you're only X many strokes back, so you're probably going to win the tournament." And he would make this statement sound completely logical, not rah-rah in any way.

That is our little phone routine on the eve of final rounds. The main value of it is that it allows me to quit thinking about the round I played that day. I usually fall asleep immediately after hanging up with him. At that point, I know for certain that I haven't missed anything or failed to notice something that could affect my play or my strategy. We go over what happened and then we shut the book on that round, and tomorrow is all that matters. These talks give me a lot of assurance that I'm doing the right thing, and that's really all I need. I can do the rest.

During my career at Ohio State, I experienced two highlights that occurred apart from NCAA competition. I won the Illinois State Amateur Championship twice, in 2013 and 2015. I was still in the early stages of my swing overhaul when I won the 2013 State Am, so I took a lot of satisfaction in that victory. Two years later, when I was in contention to possibly win that title a second time, something interesting happened. I was warming up for my round, and my normal fiery attitude wasn't there. I was looking around for the chip on my shoulder that I had become so used to, and I could not find it. My intense hatred of losing wasn't rising up inside me either.

Something had clicked or shifted. This happened either during or just after my conversation with John on the eve of the final day. For all the value John placed on my intense, basically cocky way of competing, his intuition told him there was another way for me to go. Possibly he was strategizing around the fact that it's 36 holes of play in one day, to finish up. Whatever it was, he started talking to me about the day ahead in a very calm way. "You've done this already, Tee-K," he told me. "You'll be on the golf course tomorrow with players who are trying to do something they've never done, win this championship. Those players will be wondering if they have what it takes. You won't be wondering that."

Going into the final day, I was a couple of strokes back and the way we were talking, you would have thought I had a solid lead. In John's mind, everything was positioned for me to win. The planets were all lined up. And before long that's how I felt, too.

It was a whole new concept and experience of patience, something I was never expecting to learn.

I went out and competed in an emotional condition I had never felt before. Instead of fiery confidence, my trademark, I felt a quiet, serene and very powerful self-assurance. It was a completely new feeling to have that calm come over me. John told me later that even though it had never happened before, he recognized that I had it in me somewhere and he saw a chance to help me invoke that inner state. On the back nine of the second 18, I needed to make a charge, and I had the energy and focus and confidence to do it. When regulation play ended, I was in a two-man playoff, which I was able to win.

At the end of that long day, I was holding my second Illinois Amateur trophy, and I had something else too: A new and very empowering way of harnessing my intensity and my desire in competition. It was a whole new concept and experience of patience, something I was never expecting to learn.

During college, I always seemed to play my best in the summertime when I was immersed in the TPS System. I never felt I was able to bring that game to the college season. I absolutely love Ohio State but it presented a challenge—a seven-hour drive from TPS. When senior year came around, I knew I needed to make an adjustment if I wanted to cap off my career by making

All-American. I once again needed to "S**t or get of the pot," as John put it.

John and I set a strategy that I would get back and see him periodically through the season. That's a tough sacrifice for a college kid who loved the football games and experiencing all that college offered on the weekends, but my desire to make the All-American wall at Ohio State motivated me to stick to the plan. So, on weekends, I would get home as much as possible. There was nothing new in our work together, no magic bullet, just a steady continuance of what we had done since I was 15. And it really clicked.

The place this phase of my training came together was the Lone Star Invitational in San Antonio where I achieved my first collegiate victory. It was special because it made me believe I could do it. I continued to train hard and as a result, I played steady all year and earned an individual regional bid. I knew this was my shot. I knew if I won, I would earn a trip to the nationals and have the opportunity to become an All-American.

"Drill it out on the range and
beat the game you brought."

The tournament was at Blackwolf Run in Wisconsin, which gave me the opportunity to stop in Chicago and see John on my way up to Wisconsin. At the time, my swing felt off and I was hitting this huge hook. I did not feel confident at all. I remember telling John, please give me something in the way of a swing feel to get through the week. He responded the way he always does, by telling me that quick fixes never hold up under pressure, and in order for me to play my best, I needed to stick to the strategy we've always relied on, "Drill it out on the range and beat the game you brought."

He gave me a couple new drills to do for the week to neutralize my pronounced hook, and I got after it. My practice round was a disaster but as the week went on, the drills started taking hold. John kept telling me it's a blessing in disguise when you don't feel great about your swing because when your swing is little off, your mind naturally gravitates towards a better scoring mentality, almost out of a survival instinct. He said that if I stuck to the plan, we could end up with a perfect-storm scenario: being in the optimal scoring mindset with my swing getting more neutral each day from the drills.

> What I needed was the full belief that my golf swing was part of my DNA, part of who I am at the deepest level.

Yet again, he was right. Suddenly I was striking it as pure as ever, and at the same time being stingy with my strokes. My concentration was 100% on scoring strategy; not one swing thought came into my head. I was in the zone.

As I stood next to my ball in the fairway on No. 18, I knew that a par would win me the tournament. All down the right side was water, and bunkers guarded the green to the left. I would have to fit my approach between the hazards and drop it on the green to finish the job. In that situation, the adrenaline is pumping and your body feels like it isn't your own. If you let your thoughts and mental images slip into the future, there is no way you are going to execute. The only place to be is in the present moment.

And in that moment, it became clear to me why John would never give us quick fixes for our swing mechanics. Quick fixes, when you come down to it, are artificial. They are basically a mental crutch—a story you make up about how and why you'll be able to perform. What I needed was the full belief that my golf swing was part of my DNA, part of who I am at the deepest level. I was able to summon that belief, which allowed me to step up and hit the purest shot I hit all week. When it came to rest on the putting surface, that was it. I had accomplished what I set out to accomplish years ago. My dream of becoming an All-American was a reality.

I see myself as living proof that you can reach any goal you set as long as you're willing to work hard, and you surround yourself with an effective support system. You've got a big advantage if you've got someone who cares enough about you that they will motivate you to accept things you don't want to hear. I can't say where I would be without my family and John Perna in my corner, but it's doubtful I would be a Division 1 All-American from Ohio State University who just earned his PGA Web.com Tour Card.

As many of my friends stated earlier in these pages, TPS is designed to create a competitive atmosphere. In 2015, the same year I won the State Amateur, David Cooke one-upped me and won the Illinois Open, a professional event, as an amateur. To complete this collection of stories about the TPS experience is the guy I competed against the hardest in our training, David Cooke.

David Cooke is living proof that your current situation is not your destination. He has faced more adversity than any college kid ever should. David's strength in enduring an immense personal loss has helped make him the person and player he is today. I've seen how his story touches the heart and stirs the soul of any young person who hears it. It's a true testament to the power of faith.

— J.P.

13
THE
POWER
OF
BELIEF

DAVID COOKE

2014, 2015, 2016 Wolfpack Intercollegiate Champion
(Holds Tournament record of 15-under/single-round
record of 62)
2015 Illinois Open Champion as an Amateur
(Holds Tournament record of 16-under)
2016 Academic All-ACC
2018 PGA Tour Latinoamérica Member
2019 European Tour Member
North Carolina State Graduate

I'm an athlete, who managed to become a golfer. The story of me as a tournament player doesn't even begin until my sophomore year in high school. Although it's not a long story in years, it contains a fair amount of adversity including one profound tragedy.

Everything that's happened since I gave up AAU basketball at age 16 to focus on golf comes down to belief. It demonstrates how far a person can go when a teacher they respect shows complete and unwavering belief in their potential.

That's what I got from John, beginning day one. My high school golf career, which was not at all distinguished, was over when John and I met. Up to that point, I had never broken par. I could hit the ball a long way, that was about it. I hit every club in the bag one set yardage; I couldn't take anything off a swing to vary my distances. I wasn't a good putter or a good short-game player. From where I was at the time he and I met, the logical next step for me was enrolling in a state university somewhere to study for a business degree leaving competitive golf behind.

Four years after John became my coach, I won a professional tournament, the 2015 Illinois Open, shooting 16-under par for 54 holes as an amateur. I set three scoring records in that event and won the title by five strokes over a player on the Web.com Tour with whom I was paired in the final round.

Four years after John became my coach, I won a professional tournament.

My dream was to play college golf. But as high school graduation approached, the writing was on the wall—no coach in the country wanted me. I was devastated to realize this and totally unsure what to do. I was out of answers. I knew John's reputation as a "golf whisperer." He had a reputation for having instant success with players whom I looked up to, such as Brian Bullington and Tee-K Kelly. As I called him to book a lesson, I remember sensing that this was my last resort. If nothing came of it, I would be heading down a path very different from the one that I'd always envisioned for myself.

John and I stood on his lesson tee for quite a while. We talked about where my game was and where it might go. He advised me to stay home for a gap year and enroll in community college, which I did. He told me I could train with his elite high school players, and he would do his best to get me to the point where a good golf program would consider me.

John was frank with me about how much improvement this would take. He told me I had a poor understanding of the golf swing, and my shotmaking skills were minimal. He did say that I struck him as serious-minded, as well as highly competitive. He said he could tell I sincerely loved the game of golf, which mattered a lot to him. Most important in his view was that I did possess raw talent. After two sessions, he looked me in the eye and told me I was as talented as any golfer he had ever seen, on or off the PGA Tour. He said that if we worked together, my program would not be designed just to get me a Division 1 college golf scholarship, it would be about preparing me for the PGA Tour.

It was a pretty amazing statement. I didn't understand how or why he could say what he said, but I couldn't discredit his comments given how straightforward he'd been and how seriously he spoke. His style is that he says what needs to be said, however difficult that might be. And again, I had nothing to lose at that point. I instinctively put my trust in him. As time went by, that trust only got deeper.

By September, we were well into my training process following the TPS Elite training protocol John had designed. He talked a lot about my need to recognize the performance standards of a golfer with tour aspirations and through his coaching, I did indeed develop very high expectations for my play. A certain approach shot with a certain club from a particular distance had to set up an eight-footer not a 15-footer, that kind of thing. He made sure I understood the importance of self-management and course management. His course-management system was game-changing for me. It's like an honors course in golf IQ. I needed to learn how to make birdies in a lot of different ways and how to eliminate bogeys. John would always say, "It's much easier to not lose strokes than it is to gain them." I had to learn the right way to get around the golf course taking hazards and awkward positions out of play. It was true all-around golf coaching as opposed to just golf-swing instruction.

My program included 90 to120 minutes of putting drills every day, along with very extensive chipping drills. "Don't miss any days," John told me. "If it's raining, remember that college golf teams play tournaments in the rain. So why wouldn't you do your drills in the rain?" One drill I constantly did was the one-foot chipping and pitching drill. You drop your right foot behind your left foot and balance on the left foot—front foot for a righty—and hit a long series of short shots from that position. It really helps to control your low point and trains your pivot to move in the correct sequence. It does an amazing job of allowing you to feel solid contact.

I had a putting drill where I would putt with just my left hand on the grip, then just the right hand, then both hands—25 putts left-hand-only, 25 right-hand-only, then 50 putts with both hands. He gave me drills for everything—putting, short game, wedge shots, ball-striking. Every drill had a goal, and I was required to reach that goal before I could go home. Golf practice for me could last three hours or it could last all day.

I got the idea to keep a journal of my practice sessions, and I think John was impressed by that. The year went along, and my skills improved noticeably. I had found it difficult at the beginning to be staying at home, attending community college while all my friends were away on some campus having fun and feeling grown-up. It was embarrassing to me, as though I had screwed up in high school when the fact was I had worked very hard on my academics. On top of that, I was training with all these high school kids in John's elite program. Every day was a reminder that I wasn't where I wanted to be. As the months went by, however, my sense of myself and what I was doing changed. I stopped worrying about being embarrassed or made fun of. I recognized how valuable this year was turning out to be.

I got the idea to keep a journal of my practice sessions.

Meanwhile, John was using his contacts and relationships with college coaches to try and get me an opportunity somewhere. I don't know if I was working harder on my drills or he was working harder to persuade some coach somewhere to consider me. Finally, we got word back from Purdue University, the golf coach there said he would take me as a walk-on. I was thrilled to be going to Purdue and made an even deeper commitment to work within the program John had given me so that I could continue improving. Considering where I had come from, it was a miracle that I would be headed off to play high-level Division 1 golf.

Even more surprising was to find out, when I got to Purdue, that I could hold my own with most of the other players on the team. This was dramatic proof of how well the TPS training systems work. I loved Purdue from the day I arrived on campus and felt I could have a good career there, although it still wasn't for sure that I'd be on scholarship as a sophomore.

Then certain factors came along to cause a major shift in my outlook and my plans.

It began with my younger brother, Chad, earning an athletic scholarship to play basketball at the College of Charleston. Chad and I were born a year apart and as boys, we were pretty much inseparable. We played AAU hoops together and were as close as brothers could be. We were each other's best friend. North Carolina State suddenly seemed like the right fit for me. With Chad in Charleston and me in Raleigh, it would only be a couple hours' drive to visit each other.

Another factor was my gradual acceptance of the fact that John truly believed I had the talent to play the PGA Tour. As time went on, I continued to hear his voice in my head stating very emphatically that I could do it. Once I started believing in myself as much as he did, it became obvious to me that in order to give myself the best chance to reach my potential, I needed to be practicing 12 months a year outdoors and on the golf course. Remember, I had started the game very late. I needed as much course time as possible if I was going to catch up to guys who had been competing in tournaments since they were eight or ten years old.

> John and I communicated all the time by phone, by text and through videos I would send along for him to comment on.

When I got to NC State, I found myself overwhelmed at times by the low scores some of the players were shooting. I had made progress while at Purdue, but I still had a lot to prove. As a Wolfpack sophomore, I was able to find my footing and put together a decent year. John and I communicated all the time by phone, by text and through videos I would send along for him to comment on. But it was really in my junior year that the training took hold. I played well in most of our tournaments that fall and was able to win two individual titles. It felt like the stars were lining up for me.

I flew back to Chicago for Christmas junior year feeling

good about the decisions I'd made and how far I had come with my golf. It was great to be home with my family on a break from school and especially cool that Chad and I got to hang out together a lot. One day, we went to a nearby gym to shoot baskets and ended up playing in some pick-up games. Chad was one of the better players out there, and it was fun to see him compete. Midway through one of the games, he was running downcourt after a basket and for some reason he went to the floor. No one had pushed him or tripped him, he simply collapsed. We all ran over to find out what was wrong, but my brother was unresponsive. I didn't understand it at the time, but he was going into cardiac arrest.

Someone called 911 and people tried CPR but nothing seemed to help. Paramedics arrived about 15 minutes later with a defibrillator, and they rushed Chad to the hospital. In the emergency room, the doctors worked to revive him. He was coming in and out of arrest for about 90 minutes. Then it was over. They were not able to save him. He was pronounced dead right there, at age 21, due to an episode of arrhythmia. Chad had no known heart condition and had never been diagnosed with any cardiac issues. I don't need to say how devastated I was. I couldn't put it into words anyway.

Our family had three weeks to be with each other and try to somehow comprehend our loss and begin to come to grips with it. At the end of that time, I went back to college for second semester not sure if it was the right thing to do. It helped to know that Chad would have wanted me to keep moving forward, living my life. My team was very supportive, and the university provided grief counseling. There were youth ministers who would talk with me as long as I needed. I became friends with several of them as a result of this ordeal. I think about my brother Chad every single day.

A shock and a loss that painful makes you question everything. I wondered if golf would still be important to me, important enough for me to maintain the dedication that was required. When I got back home from school in May, I really took advantage of my support system with John and my fellow TPS players. John and I talked a lot, we had dinners together, we worked on the range. Chad had been my biggest fan and the one person other than John who always told me I would achieve my goals. He always said he had no doubt that he would be going to PGA Tour events to watch his brother play.

Then came the Illinois Open in late July, which I won with a final-round 63 playing against professionals.

Remembering how Chad would say that with such assurance helped me immerse myself in my TPS training. In late May, I entered the local U.S. Open qualifier and finished first. In the beginning of July, I competed in our local U.S. Amateur qualifier and won that, as well. Then came the Illinois Open in late July, which I won with a final-round 63 playing against professionals. In some ways that streak of excellent golf felt like it came out of nowhere, but you could also say it was something I had been building toward for a long time.

The 63 I shot, on a par-72 course, was not the low round of the day. That's surprising on its own, but it's even more unusual that it was another amateur who came in lower, shooting 62. And even more amazing is that it was a fellow TPS golfer, another player from John's program, Matt Weber. Matt was on scholarship at Indiana University and coming off his freshman year. He was playing in the third group out and was well into his round as I began my warmups. John was on the course following him, naturally.

I got word that Matt had gone out in 29, having birdied six of the first seven holes. There was a lot of buzz and excitement back at the range, which only increased as Matt played the back nine. By the time he walked off No. 15, there were 11 birdies on his card and people were talking about a possible 59.

When it was over, John was obviously thrilled by what Matt had done, turning in that phenomenal round and setting the course record. But he also knew how distracting and possibly disorienting it had to be for me, trying to stay focused on my own preparation while a fellow TPS player was tearing the golf course apart. John decided to take an apparent problem and turn it into something that would in fact help me.

So from his perspective, the idea that I was there to try and win the Illinois Open, outplaying a tour pro in my pairing, went out the window. It wasn't what the day was going to be about.

"Beat Matt," he told me. "Take on that challenge—shoot the low TPS round of the day." Right away I liked this idea, and beating Matt became the goal I took with me to the first tee. What it did was make things very simple and familiar. I was in TPS, Matt was in TPS, all of us have friendly rivalries with each other, this would just be more of what we did all the time.

The things John had said years earlier
about my ability now made sense to me.

I came one stroke short of achieving that goal, but in the end it didn't matter. I signed my card, stood at the presentation and savored the moment. All the reporters covering the event knew what had happened with Chad, and they wrote about it in their articles. The victory became a chance for me to dedicate something to his memory and to feel, all the more, that my brother was alongside me. It also gave me the opportunity to get exposure for the charity our family had set up in his memory.

> Once the presentation was over, John left.
> He made a point of not speaking to the media.
> He wanted all the coverage to be about me
> and our family and Chad's charity.

Standing there with my trophy, I was also aware how special it had been to break through and achieve an important win with John walking beside me. Once the presentation was over, John left. He made a point of not speaking to the media. He wanted all the coverage to be about me and our family and Chad's charity. That's just the type of person he is. He cares more about us than about himself. I think it's the reason we all love him so much. When he pushes us to achieve our goals, it's all for us, not for his own fame or financial gain. That's why, no matter how tough he is on us, we all thrive on it because we all know he has our best interests at heart.

Before that summer ended, I went down to Olympia Fields and played in the U.S. Amateur. I won my first match 3 and 2 then lost, 2 down, in the round of 32. Despite that disappointment, I could sense that I was a different golfer at this point. The things John had said years earlier about my ability now made sense to me. He and I focused on visualization and using mental images, something that is core to his approach. At NC State that year, I had three top-five finishes and won our home tournament, the Wolfpack Intercollegiate, with a tournament-record score of 15-under for 54 holes including a course record 62 in one round.

Since then, I've graduated from college, turned professional and just earned my European Tour Card. Not bad for a kid who wasn't recruited out of high school!

The story from here forward is about working toward the ultimate goal of becoming one of the best players in the world. It's not something you do without considering the adversity you're going to face, and I'm aware of that.

I'm also aware of what unshakeable belief can provide when you're on the receiving end of it. My experience has taught me that belief will beat adversity, every time.

AFTERWORD

Thank you for taking the time to read this book and learn about the Player Service. No doubt you found the voices of the young golfers who spoke in these pages to be impressive and memorable. They are the first students to train in the TPS System from high school all the way through college golf. The TPS System has produced more than 80 Division 1 golfers along with six state champions in eight years. They are all fine, intelligent, hardworking people whose friendship I will treasure as long as I live. Without their commitment and trust, there would be no TPS.

It has been my pleasure to share their stories and hopefully open your mind to our proprietary systematic training protocol. I hope this book serves as a motivator to junior golfers everywhere and outlines the attributes necessary for success in golf as well as in life. I also hope that this book inspires instructors and coaches to see what is possible if you think outside the box and create a community of learners.

If you are a golfer aspiring to develop into a player, please visit our website **www.tpsplayerservice.com** to learn more about our training options.

If you are a collegiate coach or golf instructor desiring a deeper understanding of how to utilize our system to improve performance, please apply for our certification program at **www.tpscoachservice.com**.

JOHN PERNA
Founder and President
TPS Player Service

John Perna is founder and owner-operator of the Player Service, a golf academy based just outside Chicago, Illinois. Known informally as TPS, the academy specializes in training junior golfers who aspire to play collegiate golf, collegiate golfers who aspire to become professional golfers, and professional golfers who dream of playing on the PGA Tour or the LPGA Tour. In addition to developing golfers into players, TPS is also a leader in educating college coaches and golf instructors on their proprietary training system.

TPS has experienced unprecedented success for a golf academy in a northern, short-season location. Since the 2010 launch of TPS, six of its seven original students have, by age 24, earned PGA Tour-affiliated status. TPS has developed the No. 1 ranked boy or girl in Illinois every year from 2011 through 2018. At this writing, TPS is training the No. 1 ranked boy in Illinois in the 2019, 2020, 2021 and 2022 class and the No. 1 ranked girl in Illinois in the 2020, 2021 and 2022 class. Over the past eight years, TPS has sent more than 80 players to NCAA Division 1 schools to play golf. In total, more than 100 TPS players have gone on to play collegiately.

As you'll notice in reading this book, TPS training puts a high priority on educating young players to the concepts and protocols behind all the instruction and coaching they receive. Over time they learn the "why" of their training and are able to do an extensive amount of self-coaching. This allows them, over time, to fix problems that might show up in their games and to fine tune their skills in specific areas.

Education is also the basis for the overall quality of TPS training, as represented by the long list of certifications the author has accumulated. These have been conferred upon him by the programs that top golf instructors consider most critical and valuable:

Certified Trackman University Master

Certification by The Biomechanics of Golf Program administered by the Golf Teaching and Research Center of Penn State University

Admitted to the Certified Golf Coaches Association founded and operated by Dr. Rick Jensen

Titleist Performance Institute,
Certified Golf Fitness Instructor

Dr. Kwon's Golf Biomechanics Instructor Training Program, Certified Instructor

L.A.W.S. Golf, Certified Instructor

Swing Catalyst, Certified Instructor

Bodi-Trak Golf Ground Force Mechanics,
Certified Instructor

SeeMore Putter Institute, Certified

Science & Motion Golf Putting, Certified Instructor

FCG Top 50 Elite Junior Golf Coach in USA

FCG Top 25 Elite Junior Golf Coach in USA

Golf Digest Best Young Teachers in USA

The author warmly expresses his appreciation to these people and organizations for their efforts in producing such important research, products and services in support of dedicated coaches and instructors. They perform an invaluable service to the golf profession, and to improvement-minded golfers of all skill levels.

ACKNOWLEDGEMENTS

This book could not have been written, nor could the Player Service have become a successful training academy, without the help of the many people who assisted me in my own path through competitive golf toward a career in teaching and coaching.

In that context, I wish to thank first and foremost my parents, Mike and Adelle, for sacrificing so much to afford me the privilege of chasing my passion. My gratitude also goes to my sister, Ashley, for always believing in me when I needed it most. I thank my wife, Amanda, and my children, Michael and Jack, for giving me unconditional love and support despite all the time this journey requires.

Sincere thanks to my golf mentors Doc Suttie, Rick Jensen, Lorin Anderson, Chip Brewer and, most importantly, Dan Kochevar, who not only taught me to play the game, but also encouraged and supported all my crazy visions for a special kind of golf academy.

And finally, a special thanks to David Gould, whose professional talents made this book what it is.

—*John Perna*

Made in the USA
Lexington, KY
04 May 2019